Dearest Charlie,

It's time for us to stop, draw a breath, and enjoy the ever-changing moments in nature.

It is these moments that quiet the mind.

All my love,

Diana xxx

P9-DUZ-057

"Our ability to perceive quality in nature

begins, as in art, with the pretty.

It expands through successive stages

of the beautiful to values as yet

uncaptured by language."

Aldo Leopold

A SAND COUNTY ALMANAC ILLUSTRATED

By ALDO LEOPOLD

Photographs by Tom Algire

Tamarack Press

Post Office Box 5650

Madison, Wisconsin 53705

Distributed by

Oxford University Press

London, Oxford, New York

Copyright © 1977 by Tamarack Press, a division of Wisconsin Tales and Trails, Inc., of Madison, Wisconsin. All rights reserved. No part of this work may be reproduced in any form or by any means—graphic, electronic, or mechanical, including photocopying, recording, taping, or information storage and retrieval systems—without the written consent of the publisher.

Introduction by Hal Borland copyright © 1977 by Hal Borland.

The text by Aldo Leopold is from *A Sand County Almanac with other essays on conservation from Round River* by Aldo Leopold. Copyright © 1949, 1953, 1966, renewed 1977 by Oxford University Press, Inc.

A Sand County Almanac was first published by Oxford University Press, New York, 1949. This edition is designed and produced by Tamarack Press, P.O. Box 5650, Madison, Wisconsin, and is published in association with Oxford University Press, New York, 1977.

Library of Congress Cataloging in Publication Data
Leopold, Aldo, 1886-1948
    A Sand County almanac illustrated.

    First published in 1949 under title: A Sand County almanac.
    1. Natural history—Outdoor books. 2. Nature conservation—United States. 3. Natural history—United States. I. Title.
QH81.L56 1977   500.9'73   77-22656
ISBN 0-915024-15-2

Designed by William T. Pope

Typeset by Fleetwood Graphics

Printed in the United States of America by Litho Productions, Incorporated

Acknowledgments

Grateful acknowledgment is made to the editors of the following magazines and journals who have kindly allowed to be reprinted in book form portions or all of individual articles: *Outdoor America*, "The Alder Fork"; *Wisconsin Agriculturist and Farmer*, "Bur Oak" and "Sky Dance"; *Wisconsin Conservation Bulletin*, "A Mighty Fortress," "Home Range," and "Pines above the Snow."

For Karen

In the course of my work on this book I had the help of many people. Completion of the project would have been difficult, if not impossible, without this assistance.

First I would like to thank the landowners, both on and off the Leopold Memorial Reserve, who let me tramp over their properties in pursuit of photographs. I especially want to thank Charles and Nina Bradley, for their hospitality, and Frank Terbilcox, who manages the Reserve.

Special thanks are due Virginia Kline of the University of Wisconsin Arboretum for help in the identification of the final selections for the book. To Howard Mead, who conceived of the idea for the book, to William Pope, who designed it, and to all the staff of Tamarack Press go my sincere thanks for their support and patience during the project.

Thanks must also go to my family and friends, who contributed in many ways to make my work on the project easier and more enjoyable. I especially would like to mention Don and Lynn Isherwood, of Plover, and Mary Hangartner and Bob Jaeger, of Madison, for the warm companionship they extended to me.

Finally, I would like to thank my wife, Karen, for her constant encouragement and patience, and our two children, Andrew and Sylvia, for welcoming me back home from each trip to the sand counties with such great enthusiasm.

Tom Algire

Contents

Introduction

Try as he may, man cannot totally divorce himself from his environment, the earth of his own origins. Yet he persists in insulating himself from the earth by such a prosaic, unnatural thing as pavement, and he congregates in places where such fundamental matters as rain and snow are nuisances despite all his efforts to abate them. It seems to some of us that man should be able to see grass and trees, see fields that feed him and all his kind, see hills and valleys, and know streams that flow free and clean. At the least, he should know where he lives, what particular part of the universe he inhabits, what the earth itself looks and feels like. He should know places where he can face the sky, touch the living soil, even see the stars in the darkness of night. Otherwise he becomes so ingrown, so overwhelmed by the crowd, that he forgets who he is or where he is.

That, in a large sense, is what conservationists are talking about. They insist that man should keep his hot hands off enough wild, undeveloped places to leave us room to know our natural environment. Conservation, after all, simply means to save, not to alter for some immediate purpose and create a profit that will finance further change. Basic to all of this, of course, is the arrogant belief that man owns the earth and must reshape it to his own whims and purposes. Actually man is one of the smallest minorities in the whole span of life forms, and he is here on sufferance, though he now has created the means to wipe out not only his own kind but half the other major forms of life, all in a few ghastly flashes.

There have been dissenters to this man-owns-the-earth attitude for many years, but, until we had occupied the continent and tamed the easily accessible parts of it, such dissent was largely ignored. In fact, it was practically sentimentalized by such philosophers as Emerson, who said, "He who knows what sweets and virtues are in the ground, in the waters, the plants, the heavens, and how to come to these enchantments is the rich and royal man." His language is lush and his thinking constricted by the New England scene, largely tamed. Thoreau, though possessed of a nubbin of orientalism, did have his say in simple, direct words. "In wildness," he said, "is the preservation of the world." And, "Nowadays almost all man's improvements, so called, as the building of houses and the cutting down of the forest and of all large trees, simply deform the landscape and make it more and more tame and cheap."

But it wasn't until this century, when the problem was sufficiently recognized, that the first natural areas were set aside for national parks and forests, that the first real conservation movement got under way. Aldo Leopold, who spent time and learned much in those forests and parks, became a spokesman whose words clarified ideas that were to shape much of today's environmental thinking. He spoke of "an environmental conscience" and, in his teaching and writing, became a kind of environmental conscience for this country.

Ecology is a tricky matter, really, and subject to all kinds of interpretation. To many of us, it really means the study or science of our surroundings, where we live. Those surroundings can be hospitable or hostile, beautiful or ugly, healthy or sick—though let's admit that all these terms are subjective. But what conservationists want is enough natural environment to keep reminding us of reality, natural reality, and to restore our belief in environmental integrity. The environment of land, air, and water achieves its own beauty and even a kind of hospitality for the human race by being left to organize itself and build its own special satisfactions. All it needs, really, is to be protected from man's vandal tendencies, his passion for tearing things down, his slovenly habits, which make sewers of his rivers, foul the air he breathes and the water he drinks, and poison the soil that grows his food.

Once a woodland is cut, it takes years to restore itself. Once a hill is leveled, a valley filled, or a swamp or pond drained, only time and the elements can repair the damage. Once a river is polluted, it takes an act of Congress, a presidential proclamation, twenty years, and millions of dollars to clean its waters again.

In his own foreword to this book, Leopold said, "There are some who can live without wild things, and some who cannot. These essays are the delights and dilemmas of one who cannot." And right there is the very personal reason for his strong advocacy of what some call "game management." His purpose was to preserve and restore the "wild things," and he did it by encouraging the restoration of an environment that would be a natural home and breeding place for that area's original wild life. It came close to "environmental management," though often it meant simply keeping hands off after the initial start. It did not mean releasing pen-grown birds in a hunting area two weeks before the season opens, year after year.

Conservation, I said earlier, is saving, preservation. But it is more. It is also wise use, and that brings it back, of course, to human judgment. But that use we are talking about now is by the whole ecological community; the soil, the water, the fauna and flora, and the people. People, of course, must bring both good judgment and an active conscience, and eventually they must stop being intimidated by the argument that an action is impossible if it does not yield quick profits for somebody.

Leopold was not blind to such problems. He once said, "The hope of the future lies not in curbing the influence of human occupancy—it is already too late for that—but in creating a better understanding of the extent of that influence and a new ethic for its governance."

And he also said, "Twenty centuries of 'progress' have brought the average citizen a vote, a national anthem, a Ford, a bank account, and a high opinion of himself, but not the capacity to live in high density without befouling and denuding his environment, nor a conviction that such capacity, rather than such density, is the true test of whether he is civilized."

And if that sounds cynical, I don't see how anyone with an ecological conscience could react otherwise. Yet, on the whole, Leopold was a hopeful man. I am not sure that today, even with all the conservation talk, all the environmental study and action, even at the national level, we have got very far beyond the point where spoliation is the consequence of our insistent programs to "maintain civilization." What can you do with highway builders who insist on cutting canyons through scenic hills instead of going around them in a beautiful sweep with a panorama? Who slash through a priceless woodland, whose trees it will take a century to replace, when there is an easy way around? What can you do with flood-control agencies that build dams instead of restoring upstream woodlands and other natural storage areas? Or with Army engineers who dam some of the most beautiful rivers in the world to irrigate unneeded farmland or produce hydroelectric power so people can watch color television a thousand miles away?

The list of environmental absurdities is too long to try to set down here, and too depressing. Such absurdities are consequences of the dominance of the profit motive and the human habit of conquest. They violate basic rules of living anywhere in this natural world.

All these things Aldo Leopold either knew or anticipated and warned about. He was no "conservation guru," but he pointed the way. He was, as one acquaintance said of him, "no nature-loving idealist; he was a realist in the best sense of the word. And in his own way he was hard-boiled." He certainly would be less than cordial to some of the present-day extremists. His personal stationery identified him as a "Consulting Forester," not as a conservationist or an environmental authority.

His *Sand County Almanac* is an unpretentious, more or less simple account of the outdoors and the wildlife he knew at a vacation place he chose because, as he said, he couldn't live without wild things somewhere nearby. But it is not as simple as it seems at first reading. He wrote with a pungent pen, and his words were direct, which is one reason he gained and still holds his audience. In the *Almanac's* simple stories of wildlife, there often are parables and big truths.

In a different context, however, he said, "In our attempt to make conservation easy, we have made it trivial." And he said, "It is a surprise to biological scientists to discover as a fellow explorer the conservation ecologist, seeking not new ways to squeeze wealth out of the soil, but ways to prevent the extraction of its wealth from destroying its wildlife. Seeking not the conquest, but the preservation of nature."

That is typical of his thinking. It is the attitude of today's realistic conservationists. They want to use what is needed, and use it wisely, but to save the wild areas and keep them from wanton invasions. We who believe in saving priceless natural areas hope and trust such ghastly menaces as off-road vehicles can and will be controlled. But it is on the big decisions—on land-use policies and on the enforcement of conservation regulations already available—that the really lasting answers wait. We save or we repeat the old, old pattern; invade and conquer.

Aldo Leopold, we sometimes think, should have written more. We should have more of his clear, eloquent thinking. And yet we do have his fundamental ideas the way he set them down. And we have such delightful essays as those in *Sand County Almanac*. His tragic death came at a time when he was still moderately hopeful that conservation could be accomplished, at least enough to help mankind to appreciate this world as it is, as it tries to be when man ceases his pillaging and abuse. One wonders how he would feel about conservation today.

Meanwhile, one can read the *Almanac*. That is an excellent way to make or renew acquaintance with Aldo Leopold.

Hal Borland

Foreword

There are some who can live without wild things, and some who cannot. These essays are the delights and dilemmas of one who cannot.

Like winds and sunsets, wild things were taken for granted until progress began to do away with them. Now we face the question whether a still higher 'standard of living' is worth its cost in things natural, wild, and free. For us of the minority, the opportunity to see geese is more important than television, and the chance to find a pasque-flower is a right as inalienable as free speech.

These wild things, I admit, had little human value until mechanization assured us of a good breakfast, and until science disclosed the drama of where they come from and how they live. The whole conflict thus boils down to a question of degree. We of the minority see a law of diminishing returns in progress; our opponents do not.

ʃ ʃ ʃ

One must make shift with things as they are. These essays are my shifts.

They tell what my family sees and does at its week-end refuge from too much modernity: 'the shack.' On this sand farm in Wisconsin, first worn out and then abandoned by our bigger-and-better society, we try to rebuild, with shovel and axe, what we are losing elsewhere. It is here that we seek—and still find—our meat from God.

These shack sketches are arranged seasonally as a 'Sand County Almanac.'

ʃ ʃ ʃ

Conservation is getting nowhere because it is incompatible with our Abrahamic concept of land. We abuse land because we regard it as a commodity belonging to us. When we see land as a community to which we belong, we may begin to use it with love and respect. There is no other way for land to survive the impact of mechanized man, nor for us to reap from it the esthetic harvest it is capable, under science, of contributing to culture.

That land is a community is the basic concept of ecology, but that land is to be loved and respected is an extension of ethics. That land yields a cultural harvest is a fact long known, but latterly often forgotten.

These essays attempt to weld these three concepts.

Such a view of land and people is, of course, subject to the blurs and distortions of personal experience and personal bias. But wherever the truth may lie, this much is crystal-clear: our bigger-and-better society is now like a hypochondriac, so obsessed with its own economic health as to have lost the capacity to remain healthy. The whole world is so greedy for more bathtubs that it has lost the stability necessary to build them, or even to turn off the tap. Nothing could be more salutary at this stage than a little healthy contempt for a plethora of material blessings.

Perhaps such a shift of values can be achieved by reappraising things unnatural, tame, and confined in terms of things natural, wild, and free.

Aldo Leopold

Madison, Wisconsin
4 March 1948

January

January Thaw

Each year, after the midwinter blizzards, there comes a night of thaw when the tinkle of dripping water is heard in the land. It brings strange stirrings, not only to creatures abed for the night, but to some who have been asleep for the winter. The hibernating skunk, curled up in his deep den, uncurls himself and ventures forth to prowl the wet world, dragging his belly in the snow. His track marks one of the earliest datable events in that cycle of beginnings and ceasings which we call a year.

The track is likely to display an indifference to mundane affairs uncommon at other seasons; it leads straight across-country, as if its maker had hitched his wagon to a star and dropped the reins. I follow, curious to deduce his state of mind and appetite, and destination if any.

𝒥 𝒥 𝒥

The months of the year, from January up to June, are a geometric progression in the abundance of distractions. In January one may follow a skunk track, or search for bands on the chickadees, or see what young pines the deer have browsed, or what muskrat houses the mink have dug, with only an occasional and mild digression into other doings. January observation can be almost as simple and peaceful as snow, and almost as continuous as cold. There is time not only to see who has done what, but to speculate why.

∂ ∂ ∂

A meadow mouse, startled by my approach, darts damply across the skunk track. Why is he abroad in daylight? Probably because he feels grieved about the thaw. Today his maze of secret tunnels, laboriously chewed through the matted grass under the snow, are tunnels no more, but only paths exposed to public view and ridicule. Indeed the thawing sun has mocked the basic premises of the microtine economic system!

The mouse is a sober citizen who knows that grass grows in order that mice may store it as underground haystacks, and that snow falls in order that mice may build subways from stack to stack: supply, demand, and transport all neatly organized. To the mouse, snow means freedom from want and fear.

∂ ∂ ∂

A rough-legged hawk comes sailing over the meadow ahead. Now he stops, hovers like a kingfisher, and then drops like a feathered bomb into the marsh. He does not rise again, so I am sure he has caught, and is now eating, some worried mouse-engineer who could not wait until night to inspect the damage to his well-ordered world.

The rough-leg has no opinion why grass grows, but he is well aware that snow melts in order that hawks may again catch mice. He came down out of the Arctic in the hope of thaws, for to him a thaw means freedom from want and fear.

꧂ ꧂ ꧂

The skunk track enters the woods, and crosses a glade where the rabbits have packed down the snow with their tracks, and mottled it with pinkish urinations. Newly exposed oak seedlings have paid for the thaw with their newly barked stems. Tufts of rabbit-

hair bespeak the year's first battles among the amorous bucks. Further on I find a bloody spot, encircled by a wide-sweeping arc of owl's wings. To this rabbit the thaw brought freedom from want, but also a reckless abandonment of fear. The owl has reminded him that thoughts of spring are no substitute for caution.

ℐ ℐ ℐ

The skunk track leads on, showing no interest in possible food, and no concern over the rompings or retributions of his neighbors. I wonder what he has on his mind; what got him out of bed? Can one impute romantic motives to this corpulent fellow, dragging his ample beltline through the slush? Finally the track enters a pile of driftwood, and does not emerge. I hear the tinkle of dripping water among the logs, and I fancy the skunk hears it too. I turn homeward, still wondering.

February

Good Oak

There are two spiritual dangers in not owning a farm. One is the danger of supposing that breakfast comes from the grocery, and the other that heat comes from the furnace.

To avoid the first danger, one should plant a garden, preferably where there is no grocer to confuse the issue.

To avoid the second, he should lay a split of good oak on the andirons, preferably where there is no furnace, and let it warm his shins while a February blizzard tosses the trees outside. If one has cut, split, hauled, and piled his own good oak, and let his mind work the while, he will remember much about where the heat comes from, and with a wealth of detail denied to those who spend the week end in town astride a radiator.

♫ ♫ ♫

The particular oak now aglow on my andirons grew on the bank of the old emigrant road where it climbs the sandhill. The stump, which I measured upon felling the tree, has a diameter of 30 inches. It shows 80 growth rings, hence the seedling from which it originated must have laid its first ring of wood in 1865, at the end of the Civil War. But I know from the history of present seedlings that no oak grows above the reach of rabbits without a decade or more of getting girdled each winter, and re-sprouting during the following summer. Indeed, it is all too clear that every surviving oak is the product either of rabbit negligence or of rabbit scarcity. Some day some patient botanist will draw a frequency curve of oak birth-years, and show that the curve humps every ten years, each hump originating from a low in the ten-year rabbit cycle. (A fauna and flora, by this very process of perpetual battle within and among species, achieve collective immortality.)

It is likely, then, that a low in rabbits occurred in the middle 'sixties, when my oak began to lay on annual rings, but that the acorn that produced it fell during the preceding decade, when the covered wagons were still passing over my road into the Great Northwest. It may have been the wash and wear of the emigrant traffic that bared this roadbank, and thus enabled this particular acorn to spread its first leaves to the sun. Only one acorn in a thousand ever grew large enough to fight rabbits; the rest were drowned at birth in the prairie sea.

It is a warming thought that this one wasn't, and thus lived to garner eighty years of June sun. It is this sunlight that is now being released, through the intervention of my axe and saw, to warm my shack and my spirit through eighty gusts of blizzard. And with each gust a wisp of smoke from my chimney bears witness, to whomsoever it may concern, that the sun did not shine in vain.

My dog does not care where heat comes from, but he cares ardently that it come, and soon. Indeed he considers my ability to make it come as something magical, for when I rise in the cold black pre-dawn and kneel shivering by the hearth making a fire, he pushes himself blandly between me and the kindling splits I have laid on the ashes, and

I must touch a match to them by poking it between his legs. Such faith, I suppose, is the kind that moves mountains.

It was a bolt of lightning that put an end to wood-making by this particular oak. We were all awakened, one night in July, by the thunderous crash; we realized that the bolt must have hit near by, but, since it had not hit us, we all went back to sleep. Man brings all things to the test of himself, and this is notably true of lightning.

Next morning, as we strolled over the sandhill rejoicing with the cone-flowers and the prairie clovers over their fresh accession of rain, we came upon a great slab of bark freshly torn from the trunk of the roadside oak. The trunk showed a long spiral scar of barkless sapwood, a foot wide and not yet yellowed by the sun. By the next day the leaves had wilted, and we knew that the lightning had bequeathed to us three cords of prospective fuel wood.

We mourned the loss of the old tree, but knew that a dozen of its progeny standing straight and stalwart on the sands had already taken over its job of wood-making.

We let the dead veteran season for a year in the sun it could no longer use, and then on a crisp winter's day we laid a newly filed saw to its bastioned base. Fragrant little chips of history spewed from the saw cut, and accumulated on the snow before each kneeling sawyer. We sensed that these two piles of sawdust were something more than wood: that they were the integrated transect of a century; that our saw was biting its way, stroke by stroke, decade by decade, into the chronology of a lifetime, written in concentric annual rings of good oak.

෴ ෴ ෴

It took only a dozen pulls of the saw to transect the few years of our ownership, during which we had learned to love and cherish this farm. Abruptly we began to cut the years of our predecessor the bootlegger, who hated this farm, skinned it of residual fertility, burned its farmhouse, threw it back into the lap of the County (with delinquent taxes to boot), and then disappeared among the landless anonymities of the Great Depression. Yet the oak had laid down good wood for him; his sawdust was as fragrant, as sound, and as pink as our own. An oak is no respecter of persons.

The reign of the bootlegger ended sometime during the dust-bowl drouths of 1936, 1934, 1933, and 1930. Oak smoke from his still and peat from burning marshlands must have clouded the sun in those years, and alphabetical conservation was abroad in the land, but the sawdust shows no change.

Rest! cries the chief sawyer, and we pause for breath.

ʃ ʃ ʃ

Now our saw bites into the 1920's, the Babbittian decade when everything grew bigger and better in heedlessness and arrogance—until 1929, when stock markets crumpled. If the oak heard them fall, its wood gives no sign. Nor did it heed the Legislature's several protestations of love for trees: a National Forest and a forest-crop law in 1927, a great refuge on the Upper Mississippi bottomlands in 1924, and a new forest policy in 1921. Neither did it notice the demise of the state's last marten in 1925, nor the arrival of its first starling in 1923.

In March 1922, the 'Big Sleet' tore the neighboring elms limb from limb, but there is no sign of damage to our tree. What is a ton of ice, more or less, to a good oak?

Rest! cries the chief sawyer, and we pause for breath.

ʃ ʃ ʃ

Now the saw bites into 1910-20, the decade of the drainage dream, when steam shovels sucked dry the marshes of central Wisconsin to make farms, and made ash-

heaps instead. Our marsh escaped, not because of any caution or forbearance among engineers, but because the river floods it each April, and did so with a vengeance—perhaps a defensive vengeance—in the years 1913-16. The oak laid on wood just the same, even in 1915, when the Supreme Court abolished the state forests and Governor Phillip pontificated that 'state forestry is not a good business proposition.' (It did not occur to the Governor that there might be more than one definition of what is good, and even of what is business. It did not occur to him that while the courts were writing one definition of goodness in the law books, fires were writing quite another one on the face of the land. Perhaps, to be a governor, one must be free from doubt on such matters.)

While forestry receded during this decade, game conservation advanced. In 1916 pheasants became successfully established in Waukesha County; in 1915 a federal law prohibited spring shooting; in 1913 a state game farm was started; in 1912 a 'buck law' protected female deer; in 1911 an epidemic of refuges spread over the state. 'Refuge' became a holy word, but the oak took no heed.

Rest! cries the chief sawyer, and we pause for breath.

𝒥 𝒥 𝒥

Now we cut 1910, when a great university president published a book on conservation, a great sawfly epidemic killed millions of tamaracks, a great drouth burned the pineries, and a great dredge drained Horicon Marsh.

We cut 1909, when smelt were first planted in the Great Lakes, and when a wet summer induced the Legislature to cut the forest-fire appropriations.

We cut 1908, a dry year when the forests burned fiercely, and Wisconsin parted with its last cougar.

We cut 1907, when a wandering lynx, looking in the wrong direction for the promised land, ended his career among the farms of Dane County.

We cut 1906, when the first state forester took office, and fires burned 17,000 acres in these sand counties; we cut 1905 when a great flight of goshawks came out of the North and ate up the local grouse (they no doubt perched in this tree to eat some of mine). We cut 1902-3, a winter of bitter cold; 1901, which brought the most intense drouth of record (rainfall only 17 inches); 1900, a centennial year of hope, of prayer, and the usual annual ring of oak.

Rest! cries the chief sawyer, and we pause for breath.

꙰ ꙰ ꙰

Now our saw bites into the 1890's, called gay by those whose eyes turn cityward rather than landward. We cut 1899, when the last passenger pigeon collided with a charge of shot near Babcock, two counties to the north; we cut 1898 when a dry fall, followed by a snowless winter, froze the soil seven feet deep and killed the apple trees; 1897, another drouth year, when another forestry commission came into being; 1896, when 25,000 prairie chickens were shipped to market from the village of Spooner alone; 1895, another year of fires; 1894, another drouth year; and 1893, the year of 'The Bluebird Storm,' when a March blizzard reduced the migrating bluebirds to near-zero. (The first bluebirds always alighted in this oak, but in the middle 'nineties it must have gone without.) We cut 1892, another year of fires; 1891, a low in the grouse cycle; and 1890, the year of the Babcock Milk Tester, which enabled Governor Heil to boast, half a century later, that Wisconsin is America's Dairyland. The motor licenses which now parade that boast were then not foreseen, even by Professor Babcock.

It was likewise in 1890 that the largest pine rafts in history slipped down the Wisconsin

River in full view of my oak, to build an empire of red barns for the cows of the prairie states. Thus it is that good pine now stands between the cow and the blizzard, just as good oak stands between the blizzard and me.

Rest! cries the chief sawyer, and we pause for breath.

𝄢 𝄢 𝄢

Now our saw bites into the 1880's; into 1889, a drouth year in which Arbor Day was first proclaimed; into 1887, when Wisconsin appointed its first game wardens; into 1886, when the College of Agriculture held its first short course for farmers; into 1885, preceded by a winter 'of unprecedented length and severity'; into 1883, when Dean W. H. Henry reported that the spring flowers at Madison bloomed 13 days later than average; into 1882, the year Lake Mendota opened a month late following the historic 'Big Snow' and bitter cold of 1881-2.

It was likewise in 1881 that the Wisconsin Agricultural Society debated the question, 'How do you account for the second growth of black oak timber that has sprung up all over the country in the last thirty years?' My oak was one of these. One debater claimed spontaneous generation, another claimed regurgitation of acorns by southbound pigeons.

Rest! cries the chief sawyer, and we pause for breath.

✐ ✐ ✐

Now our saw bites the 1870's, the decade of Wisconsin's carousal in wheat. Monday morning came in 1879, when chinch bugs, grubs, rust, and soil exhaustion finally convinced Wisconsin farmers that they could not compete with the virgin prairies further west in the game of wheating land to death. I suspect that this farm played its share in the game, and that the sand blow just north of my oak had its origin in over-wheating.

This same year of 1879 saw the first planting of carp in Wisconsin, and also the first arrival of quack-grass as a stowaway from Europe. On 27 October 1879, six migrating prairie chickens perched on the rooftree of the German Methodist Church in Madison, and took a look at the growing city. On 8 November the markets at Madison were reported to be glutted with ducks at 10 cents each.

In 1878 a deer hunter from Sauk Rapids remarked prophetically, 'The hunters promise to outnumber the deer.'

On 10 September 1877, two brothers, shooting Muskego Lake, bagged 210 blue-winged teal in one day.

In 1876 came the wettest year of record; the rainfall piled up 50 inches. Prairie chickens declined, perhaps owing to hard rains.

In 1875 four hunters killed 153 prairie chickens at York Prairie, one county to the eastward. In the same year the U.S. Fish Commission planted Atlantic salmon in Devil's Lake, 10 miles south of my oak.

In 1874 the first factory-made barbed wire was stapled to oak trees; I hope no such artifacts are buried in the oak now under saw!

In 1873 one Chicago firm received and marketed 25,000 prairie chickens. The Chicago trade collectively bought 600,000 at $3.25 per dozen.

In 1872 the last wild Wisconsin turkey was killed, two counties to the southwest.

It is appropriate that the decade ending the pioneer carousal in wheat should likewise have ended the pioneer carousal in pigeon blood. In 1871, within a 50-mile triangle spreading northwestward from my oak, 136 million pigeons are estimated to have nested, and some may have nested in it, for it was then a thrifty sapling 20 feet tall. Pigeon hunters by scores plied their trade with net and gun, club and salt lick, and trainloads of prospective pigeon pie moved southward and eastward toward the cities. It was the last big nesting in Wisconsin, and nearly the last in any state.

This same year 1871 brought other evidence of the march of empire: the Peshtigo Fire, which cleared a couple of counties of trees and soil, and the Chicago Fire, said to have started from the protesting kick of a cow.

In 1870 the meadow mice had already staged their march of empire; they ate up the young orchards of the young state, and then died. They did not eat my oak, whose bark was already too tough and thick for mice.

It was likewise in 1870 that a market gunner boasted in the *American Sportsman* of killing 6000 ducks in one season near Chicago.

Rest! cries the chief sawyer, and we pause for breath.

✑ ✑ ✑

Our saw now cuts the 1860's, when thousands died to settle the question: Is the man-man community lightly to be dismembered? They settled it, but they did not see, nor do we yet see, that the same question applies to the man-land community.

This decade was not without its gropings toward the larger issue. In 1867 Increase A. Lapham induced the State Horticultural Society to offer prizes for forest plantations. In 1866 the last native Wisconsin elk was killed. The saw now severs 1865, the pith-year of our oak. In that year John Muir offered to buy from his brother, who then owned the home farm thirty miles east of my oak, a sanctuary for the wildflowers that had gladdened his youth. His brother declined to part with the land, but he could not suppress the idea: 1865 still stands in Wisconsin history as the birth-year of mercy for things natural, wild, and free.

We have cut the core. Our saw now reverses its orientation in history; we cut backward across the years, and outward toward the far side of the stump. At last there is a tremor in the great trunk; the saw-kerf suddenly widens; the saw is quickly pulled as the sawyers spring backward to safety; all hands cry 'Timber!'; my oak leans, groans, and crashes with earth-shaking thunder, to lie prostrate across the emigrant road that gave it birth.

✑ ✑ ✑

Now comes the job of making wood. The maul rings on steel wedges as the sections of trunk are up-ended one by one, only to fall apart in fragrant slabs to be corded by the roadside.

There is an allegory for historians in the diverse functions of saw, wedge, and axe.

The saw works only across the years, which it must deal with one by one, in sequence. From each year the raker teeth pull little chips of fact, which accumulate in little piles, called sawdust by woodsmen and archives by historians; both judge the character of what lies within by the character of the samples thus made visible without. It is not until the transect is completed that the tree falls, and the stump yields a collective view of a century. By its fall the tree attests the unity of the hodge-podge called history.

The wedge, on the other hand, works only in radial splits; such a split yields a collective view of all the years at once, or no view at all, depending on the skill with which the plane of the split is chosen. (If in doubt, let the section season for a year until a crack develops. Many a hastily driven wedge lies rusting in the woods, embedded in un-splittable cross-grain.)

The axe functions only at an angle diagonal to the years, and this only for the peripheral rings of the recent past. Its special function is to lop limbs, for which both saw and wedge are useless.

The three tools are requisite to good oak, and to good history.

⁄⁄ ⁄⁄ ⁄⁄

These things I ponder as the kettle sings, and the good oak burns to red coals on white ashes. Those ashes, come spring, I will return to the orchard at the foot of the sandhill. They will come back to me again, perhaps as red apples, or perhaps as a spirit of enterprise in some fat October squirrel, who, for reasons unknown to himself, is bent on planting acorns.

March

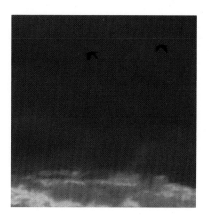

The Geese Return

One swallow does not make a summer, but one skein of geese, cleaving the murk of a March thaw, is the spring.

A cardinal, whistling spring to a thaw but later finding himself mistaken, can retrieve his error by resuming his winter silence. A chipmunk, emerging for a sunbath but finding a blizzard, has only to go back to bed. But a migrating goose, staking two hundred miles of black night on the chance of finding a hole in the lake, has no easy chance for retreat. His arrival carries the conviction of a prophet who has burned his bridges.

A March morning is only as drab as he who walks in it without a glance skyward, ear cocked for geese. I once knew an educated lady, banded by Phi Beta Kappa, who told me that she had never heard or seen the geese that twice a year proclaim the revolving seasons to her well-insulated roof. Is education possibly a process of trading awareness for things of lesser worth? The goose who trades his is soon a pile of feathers.

The geese that proclaim the seasons to our farm are aware of many things, including the Wisconsin statutes. The southbound November flocks pass over us high and haughty, with scarcely a honk of recognition for their favorite sandbars and sloughs. 'As a crow flies' is crooked compared with their undeviating aim at the nearest big lake twenty miles to the south, where they loaf by day on broad waters and filch corn by night from the freshly cut stubbles. November geese are aware that every marsh and pond bristles from dawn till dark with hopeful guns.

March geese are a different story. Although they have been shot at most of the winter, as attested by their buckshot-battered pinions, they know that the spring truce is now in effect. They wind the oxbows of the river, cutting low over the now gunless points and islands, and gabbling to each sandbar as to a long-lost friend. They weave low over the marshes and meadows, greeting each newly melted puddle and pool. Finally, after a few *pro-forma* circlings of our marsh, they set wing and glide silently to the pond, black landing-gear lowered and rumps white against the far hill. Once touching water, our newly arrived guests set up a honking and splashing that shakes the last thought of winter out of the brittle cattails. Our geese are home again!

It is at this moment of each year that I wish I were a muskrat, eye-deep in the marsh.

Once the first geese are in, they honk a clamorous invitation to each migrating flock, and in a few days the marsh is full of them. On our farm we measure the amplitude of our spring by two yardsticks: the number of pines planted, and the number of geese that stop. Our record is 642 geese counted in on 11 April 1946.

As in fall, our spring geese make daily trips to corn, but these are no surreptitious sneakings-out by night; the flocks move noisily to and from corn stubbles through the day. Each departure is preceded by loud gustatory debate, and each return by an even louder one. The returning flocks, once thoroughly at home, omit their pro-forma circlings of the marsh. They tumble out of the sky like maple leaves, side-slipping right and left to lose altitude, feet spraddled toward the shouts of welcome below. I suppose the ensuing gabble deals with the merits of the day's dinner. They are now eating the waste corn that the snow blanket has protected over winter from corn-seeking crows, cottontails, meadow mice, and pheasants.

It is a conspicuous fact that the corn stubbles selected by geese for feeding are usually those occupying former prairies. No man knows whether this bias for prairie corn reflects some superior nutritional value, or some ancestral tradition transmitted from generation to generation since the prairie days. Perhaps it reflects the simpler fact that prairie cornfields tend to be large. If I could understand the thunderous debates that precede and follow these daily excursions to corn, I might soon learn the reason for the prairie-bias. But I cannot, and I am well content that it should remain a mystery. What a dull world if we knew all about geese!

In thus watching the daily routine of a spring goose convention, one notices the prevalence of singles—lone geese that do much flying about and much talking. One is apt to impute a disconsolate tone to their honkings, and to jump to the conclusion that they are broken-hearted widowers, or mothers hunting lost children. The seasoned ornithologist knows, however, that such subjective interpretation of bird behavior is risky. I long tried to keep an open mind on the question.

After my students and I had counted for half a dozen years the number of geese

comprising a flock, some unexpected light was cast on the meaning of lone geese. It was found by mathematical analysis that flocks of six or multiples of six were far more frequent than chance alone would dictate. In other words, goose flocks are families, or aggregations of families, and lone geese in spring are probably just what our fond imaginings had first suggested. They are bereaved survivors of the winter's shooting, searching in vain for their kin. Now I am free to grieve with and for the lone honkers.

It is not often that cold-potato mathematics thus confirms the sentimental promptings of the bird-lover.

On April nights when it has become warm enough to sit outdoors, we love to listen to the proceedings of the convention in the marsh. There are long periods of silence when one hears only the winnowing of snipe, the hoot of a distant owl, or the nasal clucking of some amorous coot. Then, of a sudden, a strident honk resounds, and in an instant pandemonium echoes. There is a beating of pinions on water, a rushing of dark prows propelled by churning paddles, and a general shouting by the onlookers of a vehement controversy. Finally some deep honker has his last word, and the noise subsides to that half-audible small-talk that seldom ceases among geese. Once again, I would I were a muskrat!

By the time the pasques are in full bloom our goose convention dwindles, and before May our marsh is once again a mere grassy wetness, enlivened only by redwings and rails.

꧁ ꧁ ꧁

It is an irony of history that the great powers should have discovered the unity of nations at Cairo in 1943. The geese of the world have had that notion for a longer time, and each March they stake their lives on its essential truth.

In the beginning there was only the unity of the Ice Sheet. Then followed the unity of the March thaw, and the northward hegira of the international geese. Every March since the Pleistocene, the geese have honked unity from China Sea to Siberian Steppe, from Euphrates to Volga, from Nile to Murmansk, from Lincolnshire to Spitsbergen. Every March since the Pleistocene, the geese have honked unity from Currituck to Labrador, Matamuskeet to Ungava. Horseshoe Lake to Hudson's Bay, Avery Island to Baffin Land, Panhandle to Mackenzie, Sacramento to Yukon.

By this international commerce of geese, the waste corn of Illinois is carried through the clouds to the Arctic tundras, there to combine with the waste sunlight of a nightless June to grow goslings for all the lands between. And in this annual barter of food for light, and winter warmth for summer solitude, the whole continent receives as net profit a wild poem dropped from the murky skies upon the muds of March.

April

Come High Water

The same logic that causes big rivers always to flow past big cities causes cheap farms sometimes to be marooned by spring floods. Ours is a cheap farm, and sometimes when we visit it in April we get marooned.

Not intentionally, of course, but one can, to a degree, guess from weather reports when the snows up north will melt, and one can estimate how many days it takes for the flood to run the gauntlet of upriver cities. Thus, come Sunday evening, one must go back to town and work, but one can't. How sweetly the spreading waters murmur condolence for the wreckage they have inflicted on Monday morning dates! How deep and chesty the honkings of the geese as they cruise over cornfield after cornfield, each in process of becoming a lake. Every hundred yards some new goose flails the air as he struggles to lead the echelon in its morning survey of this new and watery world.

The enthusiasm of geese for high water is a subtle thing, and might be overlooked by those unfamiliar with goose-gossip, but the enthusiasm of carp is obvious and unmistakable. No sooner has the rising flood wetted the grass roots than here they come, rooting and wallowing with the prodigious zest of pigs turned out to pasture, flashing red tails and yellow bellies, cruising the wagon tracks and cow-paths, and shaking the reeds and bushes in their haste to explore what to them is an expanding universe. Unlike the geese and the carp, the terrestrial birds and mammals accept high water with philosophical detachment. A cardinal atop a river birch whistles loudly his claim to a territory that, but for the trees, cannot be seen to exist. A ruffed grouse drums from the flooded woods; he must be perched on the high end of his highest drumming log. Meadow-mice paddle ridgeward with the calm assurance of miniature muskrats. From the orchard bounds a deer, evicted from his usual daytime bed in the willow thickets. Everywhere are rabbits, calmly accepting quarters on our hill, which serves, in Noah's absence, for an ark.

The spring flood brings us more than high adventure; it brings likewise an unpredictable miscellany of floatable objects pilfered from upriver farms. An old board stranded on our meadow has, to us, twice the value of the same piece new from the lumberyard. Each old board has its own individual history, always unknown, but always to some degree guessable from the kind of wood, its dimensions, its nails, screws, or paint, its finish or the lack of it, its wear or decay. One can even guess, from the abrasion of its edges and ends on sandbars, how many floods have carried it in years past.

Our lumber pile, recruited entirely from the river, is thus not only a collection of personalities, but an anthology of human strivings in upriver farms and forests. The autobiography of an old board is a kind of literature not yet taught on campuses, but any riverbank farm is a library where he who hammers or saws may read at will. Come high water, there is always an accession of new books.

ꝸ ꝸ ꝸ

There are degrees and kinds of solitude. An island in a lake has one kind; but lakes have boats, and there is always the chance that one might land to pay you a visit. A peak in the clouds has another kind; but most peaks have trails, and trails have tourists.

I know of no solitude so secure as one guarded by a spring flood; nor do the geese, who have seen more kinds and degrees of aloneness than I have.

So we sit on our hill beside a new-blown pasque, and watch the geese go by. I see our road dipping gently into the waters, and I conclude (with inner glee but exterior detachment) that the question of traffic, in or out, is for this day at least, debatable only among carp.

Draba

Within a few weeks now Draba, the smallest flower that blows, will sprinkle every sandy place with small blooms.

He who hopes for spring with upturned eye never sees so small a thing as Draba. He who despairs of spring with downcast eye steps on it, unknowing. He who searches for spring with his knees in the mud finds it, in abundance.

Draba asks, and gets, but scant allowance of warmth and comfort; it subsists on the leavings of unwanted time and space. Botany books give it two or three lines, but never a plate or portrait. Sand too poor and sun too weak for bigger, better blooms are good enough for Draba. After all it is no spring flower, but only a postscript to a hope.

Draba plucks no heartstrings. Its perfume, if there is any, is lost in the gusty winds. Its color is plain white. Its leaves wear a sensible woolly coat. Nothing eats it; it is too small. No poets sing of it. Some botanist once gave it a Latin name, and then forgot it. Altogether it is of no importance—just a small creature that does a small job quickly and well.

Bur Oak

When school children vote on a state bird, flower, or tree, they are not making a decision; they are merely ratifying history. Thus history made bur oak the characteristic tree of southern Wisconsin when the prairie grasses first gained possession of the region. Bur oak is the only tree that can stand up to a prairie fire and live.

Have you ever wondered why a thick crust of corky bark covers the whole tree, even to the smallest twigs? This cork is armor. Bur oaks were the shock troops sent by the invading forest to storm the prairie; fire is what they had to fight. Each April, before the new grasses had covered the prairie with unburnable greenery, fires ran at will over the land, sparing only such old oaks as had grown bark too thick to scorch. Most of these groves of scattered veterans, known to the pioneers as 'oak openings,' consisted of bur oaks.

Engineers did not discover insulation; they copied it from these old soldiers of the prairie war. Botanists can read the story of that war for twenty thousand years. The record consists partly of pollen grains embedded in peats, partly of relic plants interned in the rear of the battle, and there forgotten. The record shows that the forest front at times retreated almost to Lake Superior; at times it advanced far to the south. At one period it advanced so far southward that spruce and other 'rear guard' species grew to and beyond the southern border of Wisconsin; spruce pollen appears at a certain level in all peat bogs of the region. But the average battle line between prairie and forest was about where it is now, and the net outcome of the battle was a draw.

One reason for this was that there were allies that threw their support first to one side, then to the other. Thus rabbits and mice mowed down the prairie herbs in summer, and in winter girdled any oak seedlings that survived the fires. Squirrels planted acorns in fall, and ate them all the rest of the year. June beetles undermined the prairie sod in their grub stage, but defoliated the oaks in their adult stage. But for this geeing and hawing of allies, and hence of the victory, we should not have today that rich mosaic of prairie and forest soils which looks so decorative on a map.

Jonathan Carver has left us a vivid word-picture of the prairie border in pre-settlement

days. On 10 October 1763, he visited Blue Mounds, a group of high hills (now wooded) near the southwestern corner of Dane County. He says:

I ascended one of the highest of these, and had an extensive view of the country. For many miles nothing was to be seen but lesser mountains, which appeared at a distance like haycocks, they being free from trees. Only a few groves of hickory, and stunted oaks, covered some of the vallies.

In the 1840's a new animal, the settler, intervened in the prairie battle. He didn't mean to, he just plowed enough fields to deprive the prairie of its immemorial ally: fire. Seedling oaks forthwith romped over the grasslands in legions, and what had been the prairie region became a region of woodlot farms. If you doubt this story, go count the rings on any set of stumps on any 'ridge' woodlot in southwest Wisconsin. All the trees except the oldest veterans date back to the 1850's and the 1860's, and this was when fires ceased on the prairie.

John Muir grew up in Marquette County during this period when new woods over-
rode the old prairies and engulfed the oak openings in thickets of saplings. In his
Boyhood and Youth he recalls that:

The uniformly rich soil of the Illinois and Wisconsin prairies produced so close and tall
a growth of grasses for fires that no tree could live on it. Had there been no fires, these
fine prairies, so marked a feature of the country, would have been covered by the

heaviest forest. As soon as the oak openings were settled, and the farmers had pre-vented running grass-fires, the grubs [roots] grew up into trees and formed tall thickets so dense that it was difficult to walk through them, and every trace of the sunny [oak] 'openings' vanished.

Thus, he who owns a veteran bur oak owns more than a tree. He owns a historical library, and a reserved seat in the theater of evolution. To the discerning eye, his farm is labeled with the badge and symbol of the prairie war.

Sky Dance

I owned my farm for two years before learning that the sky dance is to be seen over my woods every evening in April and May. Since we discovered it, my family and I have been reluctant to miss even a single performance.

The show begins on the first warm evening in April at exactly 6:50 p.m. The curtain goes up one minute later each day until 1 June, when the time is 7:50. This sliding scale is dictated by vanity, the dancer demanding a romantic light intensity of exactly 0.05 foot-candles. Do not be late, and sit quietly, lest he fly away in a huff.

The stage props, like the opening hour, reflect the temperamental demands of the performer. The stage must be an open amphitheater in woods or brush, and in its center there must be a mossy spot, a streak of sterile sand, a bare outcrop of rock, or a bare roadway. Why the male woodcock should be such a stickler for a bare dance floor puzzled me at first, but I now think it is a matter of legs. The woodcock's legs are short, and his struttings cannot be executed to advantage in dense grass or weeds, nor could his lady see them there. I have more woodcocks than most farmers because I have more mossy sand, too poor to support grass.

Knowing the place and the hour, you seat yourself under a bush to the east of the dance floor and wait, watching against the sunset for the woodcock's arrival. He flies in low from some neighboring thicket, alights on the bare moss, and at once begins the overture: a series of queer throaty *peents* spaced about two seconds apart, and sounding much like the summer call of the nighthawk.

Suddenly the peenting ceases and the bird flutters skyward in a series of wide spirals, emitting a musical twitter. Up and up he goes, the spirals steeper and smaller, the twittering louder and louder, until the performer is only a speck in the sky. Then, without warning, he tumbles like a crippled plane, giving voice in a soft liquid warble that a March bluebird might envy. At a few feet from the ground he levels off and returns to his peenting ground, usually to the exact spot where the performance began, and there resumes his peenting.

It is soon too dark to see the bird on the ground, but you can see his flights against the sky for an hour, which is the usual duration of the show. On moonlight nights, however, it may continue, at intervals, as long as the moon continues to shine.

At daybreak the whole show is repeated. In early April the final curtain falls at 5:15 a.m.; the time advances two minutes a day until June, when the performance closes for the year at 3:15. Why the disparity in sliding scale? Alas, I fear that even romance tires, for it takes only a fifth as much light to stop the sky dance at dawn as suffices to start it at sunset.

♫ ♫ ♫

It is fortunate, perhaps, that no matter how intently one studies the hundred little dramas of the woods and meadows, one can never learn all of the salient facts about any one of them. What I do not yet know about the sky dance is: where is the lady, and just what part, if any, does she play? I often see two woodcocks on a peenting ground, and the two sometimes fly together, but they never peent together. Is the second bird the hen, or a rival male?

Another unknown: is the twitter vocal, or is it mechanical? My friend, Bill Feeney, once clapped a net over a peenting bird and removed his outer primary wing feathers; thereafter the bird peented and warbled, but twittered no more. But one such experiment is hardly conclusive.

Another unknown: up to what stage of nesting does the male continue the sky dance? My daughter once saw a bird peenting within twenty yards of a nest containing hatched eggshells, but was this his lady's nest? Or is this secretive fellow possibly bigamous without our ever having found it out? These, and many other questions, remain mysteries of the deepening dusk.

The drama of the sky dance is enacted nightly on hundreds of farms, the owners of which sigh for entertainment, but harbor the illusion that it is to be sought in theaters. They live on the land, but not by the land.

The woodcock is a living refutation of the theory that the utility of a game bird is to serve as a target, or to pose gracefully on a slice of toast. No one would rather hunt woodcock in October than I, but since learning of the sky dance I find myself calling one or two birds enough. I must be sure that, come April, there be no dearth of dancers in the sunset sky.

May

Back from the Argentine

When dandelions have set the mark of May on Wisconsin pastures, it is time to listen for the final proof of spring. Sit down on a tussock, cock your ears at the sky, dial out the bedlam of meadowlarks and redwings, and soon you may hear it: the flight-song of the upland plover, just now back from the Argentine.

If your eyes are strong, you may search the sky and see him, wings aquiver, circling among the woolly clouds. If your eyes are weak, don't try it; just watch the fence posts. Soon a flash of silver will tell you on which post the plover has alighted and folded his long wings. Whoever invented the word 'grace' must have seen the wing-folding of the plover.

There he sits; his whole being says it's your next move to absent yourself from his domain. The county records may allege that you own this pasture, but the plover airily rules out such trivial legalities. He has just flown 4000 miles to reassert the title he got from the Indians, and until the young plovers are a-wing, this pasture is his, and none may trespass without his protest.

Somewhere near by, the hen plover is brooding the four large pointed eggs which will shortly hatch four precocial chicks. From the moment their down is dry, they scamper through the grass like mice on stilts, quite able to elude your clumsy efforts to catch them. At thirty days the chicks are full grown; no other fowl develops with equal speed. By August they have graduated from flying school, and on cool August nights you can hear their whistled signals as they set wing for the pampas, to prove again the

age-old unity of the Americas. Hemisphere solidarity is new among statesmen, but not among the feathered navies of the sky.

The upland plover fits easily into the agricultural countryside. He follows the black-and-white buffalo, which now pasture his prairies, and finds them an acceptable substitute for brown ones. He nests in hayfields as well as pastures, but, unlike the clumsy

pheasant, does not get caught in hay mowers. Well before the hay is ready to cut, the young plovers are a-wing and away. In farm country, the plover has only two real enemies: the gully and the drainage ditch. Perhaps we shall one day find that these are our enemies, too.

There was a time in the early 1900's when Wisconsin farms nearly lost their immemorial timepiece, when May pastures greened in silence, and August nights brought no whistled reminder of impending fall. Universal gunpowder, plus the lure of plover-on-toast for post-Victorian banquets, had taken too great a toll. The belated protection of the federal migratory bird laws came just in time.

June

The Alder Fork—A Fishing Idyl

We found the main stream so low that the teeter-snipe pattered about in what last year were trout riffles, and so warm that we could duck in its deepest pool without a shout. Even after our cooling swim, waders felt like hot tar paper in the sun.

The evening's fishing proved as disappointing as its auguries. We asked that stream for trout, and it gave us a chub. That night we sat under a mosquito smudge and debated the morrow's plan. Two hundred miles of hot, dusty road we had come, to feel again the impetuous tug of a disillusioned brook or rainbow. There were no trout. But this, we now remembered, was a stream of parts. High up near the headwaters we had once seen a fork, narrow, deep, and fed by cold springs that gurgled out under its close-hemmed walls of alder. What would a self-respecting trout do in such weather? Just what we did: go up.

In the fresh of the morning, when a hundred whitethroats had forgotten it would ever

again be anything but sweet and cool, I climbed down the dewy bank and stepped into the Alder Fork. A trout was rising just upstream. I paid out some line—wishing it would always stay thus soft and dry—and, measuring the distance with a false cast or two, laid down a spent gnat exactly a foot above his last swirl. Forgotten now were the hot miles, the mosquitoes, the ignominious chub. He took it with one great gulp, and shortly I could hear him kicking in the bed of wet alder leaves at the bottom of the creel.

Another, albeit larger, fish had meanwhile risen in the next pool, which lay at the very 'head of navigation,' for at its upper end the alders closed in solid phalanx. One bush, with its brown stem laved in the middle current, shook with a perpetual silent laughter, as if to mock at any fly that gods or men might cast one inch beyond its outermost leaf.

𝒥 𝒥 𝒥

For the duration of a cigarette I sit on a rock midstream—and watch my trout rise under his guardian bush, while my rod and line hang drying on the alders of the sunny bank. Then—for prudence' sake—a little longer. That pool is too smooth up there. A breeze is stirring and may shortly ruffle it for an instant, and thus make more deadly that perfect cast I shall shortly lay upon its bosom.

It will come—a puff strong enough to shake a brown miller off the laughing alder, and cast it upon the pool.

Ready now! Coil up the dry line and stand midstream, rod in instant readiness. It's coming—a little premonitory shiver in that aspen on the hill lets me get out half a cast, and swish it gently back and forth, ready for the main puff to hit the pool. No more than half a line, mind you! The sun is high now, and any flicking shadow overhead would forewarn my hunker of his impending fate. Now! The last three yards shoot out, the fly falls gracefully at the feet of the laughing alder—he has it! I set hard to hold him out of the jungle beyond. He rushes downstream. In a few minutes he, too, is kicking in the creel.

I sit in happy meditation on my rock, pondering, while my line dries again, upon the ways of trout and men. How like fish we are: ready, nay eager, to seize upon whatever new thing some wind of circumstance shakes down upon the river of time! And how we rue our haste, finding the gilded morsel to contain a hook. Even so, I think there is some virtue in eagerness, whether its object prove true or false. How utterly dull would be a wholly prudent man, or trout, or world! Did I say a while ago that I waited 'for prudence' sake'? That was not so. The only prudence in fishermen is that designed to set the stage for taking yet another, and perhaps a longer, chance.

Time to be at it now—they will soon stop rising. I wade waist deep to head of navigation, poke my head insolently into the shaking alder, and look within. Jungle is right! A coal-black hole above, so canopied in greenness you could not wave a fern, much less a rod, above its rushing depths. And there, almost rubbing his ribs against the dark bank, a great trout rolls lazily over as he sucks down a passing bug.

Not a chance to stalk him, even with the lowly worm. But twenty yards above I see bright sunshine on the water—another opening. Fish a dry fly downstream? It cannot, but it must, be done.

I retreat and climb the bank. Neck deep in jewel-weed and nettles, I detour through the alder thicket to the opening above. With cat-like care not to roil his majesty's bath, I step in, and stand stock-still for five minutes to let things calm down. The while, I strip out, oil, dry, and coil upon my left hand thirty feet of line. I am that far above the portal to the jungle.

Now for the long chance! I blow upon my fly to give it one last fluff, lay it on the stream at my feet, and quickly pay out coil after coil. Then, just as the line straightens out and the fly is sucked into the jungle, I walk quickly downstream, straining my eyes into the dark vault to follow its fortunes. A fleeting glimpse or two as it passes a speck of sunlight shows it still rides clear. It rounds the bend. In no time—long before the roil of my walking has betrayed the ruse—it reaches the black pool. I hear, rather than see, the rush of the great fish; I set hard, and the battle is on.

No prudent man would risk a dollar's worth of fly and leader pulling a trout upstream through the giant toothbrush of alder stems comprising the bend of that creek. But, as I said, no prudent man is a fisherman. By and by, with much cautious unraveling, I got him up into open water, and finally aboard the creel.

I shall now confess to you that none of those three trout had to be beheaded, or folded double, to fit their casket. What was big was not the trout, but the chance. What was full was not my creel, but my memory. Like the whitethroats, I had forgotten it would ever again be aught but morning on the Fork.

July

Great Possessions

One hundred and twenty acres, according to the County Clerk, is the extent of my worldly domain. But the County Clerk is a sleepy fellow, who never looks at his record books before nine o'clock. What they would show at daybreak is the question here at issue.

Books or no books, it is a fact, patent both to my dog and myself, that at daybreak I am the sole owner of all the acres I can walk over. It is not only boundaries that disappear, but also the thought of being bounded. Expanses unknown to deed or map are known to every dawn, and solitude, supposed no longer to exist in my county, extends on every hand as far as the dew can reach.

Like other great landowners, I have tenants. They are negligent about rents, but very punctilious about tenures. Indeed at every daybreak from April to July they proclaim their boundaries to each other, and so acknowledge, at least by inference, their fief-dom to me.

This daily ceremony, contrary to what you might suppose, begins with the utmost decorum. Who originally laid down its protocols I do not know. At 3:30 a.m., with such dignity as I can muster of a July morning, I step from my cabin door, bearing in either hand my emblems of sovereignty, a coffee pot and notebook. I seat myself on a bench, facing the white wake of the morning star. I set the pot beside me. I extract a cup from my shirt front, hoping none will notice its informal mode of transport. I get out my watch, pour coffee, and lay notebook on knee. This is the cue for the proclamations to begin.

At 3:35 the nearest field sparrow avows, in a clear tenor chant, that he holds the jack-pine copse north to the riverbank, and south to the old wagon track. One by one all the other field sparrows within earshot recite their respective holdings. There are no disputes, at least at this hour, so I just listen, hoping inwardly that their womenfolk acquiesce in this happy accord over the *status quo ante*.

Before the field sparrows have quite gone the rounds, the robin in the big elm warbles loudly his claim to the crotch where the icestorm tore off a limb, and all appurtenances pertaining thereto (meaning, in his case, all the angleworms in the not-very-spacious subjacent lawn).

The robin's insistent caroling awakens the oriole, who now tells the world of orioles that the pendant branch of the elm belongs to him, together with all fiber-bearing milk-weed stalks near by, all loose strings in the garden, and the exclusive right to flash like a burst of fire from one of these to another.

My watch says 3:50. The indigo bunting on the hill asserts title to the dead oak limb left by the 1936 drought, and to divers near-by bugs and bushes. He does not claim, but I think he implies, the right to out-blue all bluebirds, and all spiderworts that have turned their faces to the dawn.

Next the wren—the one who discovered the knothole in the eave of the cabin— explodes into song. Half a dozen other wrens give voice, and now all is bedlam. Grosbeaks, thrashers, yellow warblers, bluebirds, vireos, towhees, cardinals—all are at it. My solemn list of performers, in their order and time of first song, hesitates, wavers, ceases, for my ear can no longer filter out priorities. Besides, the pot is empty and the sun is about to rise. I must inspect my domain before my title runs out.

We sally forth, the dog and I, at random. He has paid scant respect to all these vocal goings-on, for to him the evidence of tenantry is not song, but scent. Any illiterate bundle of feathers, he says, can make a noise in a tree. Now he is going to translate for me the olfactory poems that who-knows-what silent creatures have written in the summer night. At the end of each poem sits the author—if we can find him. What we actually find is beyond predicting: a rabbit, suddenly yearning to be elsewhere; a woodcock, fluttering his disclaimer; a cock pheasant, indignant over wetting his feathers in the grass.

Once in a while we turn up a coon or mink, returning late from the night's foray. Sometimes we rout a heron from his unfinished fishing, or surprise a mother wood duck with her convoy of ducklings, headed full-steam for the shelter of the pickerel-weeds. Sometimes we see deer sauntering back to the thickets, replete with alfalfa blooms, veronica, and wild lettuce. More often we see only the interweaving darkened lines that lazy hoofs have traced on the silken fabric of the dew.

I can feel the sun now. The bird-chorus has run out of breath. The far clank of cowbells bespeaks a herd ambling to pasture. A tractor roars warning that my neighbor is astir. The world has shrunk to those mean dimensions known to county clerks. We turn toward home, and breakfast.

Prairie Birthday

During *every week* from April to September there are, on the average, ten wild plants coming into first bloom. In June as many as a dozen species may burst their buds on a single day. No man can heed all of these anniversaries; no man can ignore all of them. He who steps unseeing on May dandelions may be hauled up short by August ragweed pollen; he who ignores the ruddy haze of April elms may skid his car on the fallen corollas of June catalpas. Tell me of what plant-birthday a man takes notice, and I shall tell you a good deal about his vocation, his hobbies, his hay fever, and the general level of his ecological education.

ॐ ॐ ॐ

Every July I watch eagerly a certain country graveyard that I pass in driving to and from my farm. It is time for a prairie birthday, and in one corner of this graveyard lives a surviving celebrant of that once important event.

It is an ordinary graveyard, bordered by the usual spruces, and studded with the usual pink granite or white marble headstones, each with the usual Sunday bouquet of red or pink geraniums. It is extraordinary only in being triangular instead of square, and in harboring, within the sharp angle of its fence, a pin-point remnant of the native prairie on which the graveyard was established in the 1840's. Heretofore unreachable by scythe or mower, this yard-square relic of original Wisconsin gives birth, each July, to a man-high stalk of compass plant or cutleaf Silphium, spangled with saucer-sized

yellow blooms resembling sunflowers. It is the sole remnant of this plant along this highway, and perhaps the sole remnant in the western half of our county. What a thousand acres of Silphiums looked like when they tickled the bellies of the buffalo is a question never again to be answered, and perhaps not even asked.

This year I found the Silphium in first bloom on 24 July, a week later than usual; during the last six years the average date was 15 July.

When I passed the graveyard again on 3 August, the fence had been removed by a road crew, and the Silphium cut. It is easy now to predict the future; for a few years my Silphium will try in vain to rise above the mowing machine, and then it will die. With it will die the prairie epoch.

The Highway Department says that 100,000 cars pass yearly over this route during the three summer months when the Silphium is in bloom. In them must ride at least 100,000 people who have 'taken' what is called history, and perhaps 25,000 who have 'taken' what is called botany. Yet I doubt whether a dozen have seen the Silphium, and of these hardly one will notice its demise. If I were to tell a preacher of the adjoining church that the road crew has been burning history books in his cemetery, under the guise of mowing weeds, he would be amazed and uncomprehending. How could a weed be a book?

This is one little episode in the funeral of the native flora, which in turn is one episode in the funeral of the floras of the world. Mechanized man, oblivious of floras, is proud of his progress in cleaning up the landscape on which, willy-nilly, he must live out his days. It might be wise to prohibit at once all teaching of real botany and real history, lest some future citizen suffer qualms about the floristic price of his good life.

𝄞 𝄞 𝄞

Thus it comes to pass that farm neighborhoods are good in proportion to the poverty of their floras. My own farm was selected for its lack of goodness and its lack of highway; indeed my whole neighborhood lies in a backwash of the River Progress. My road is the original wagon track of the pioneers, innocent of grades or gravel, brushings or bulldozers. My neighbors bring a sigh to the County Agent. Their fencerows go unshaven for years on end. Their marshes are neither dyked nor drained. As between going fishing and going forward, they are prone to prefer fishing. Thus on week ends my floristic standard of living is that of the backwoods, while on week days I subsist as best I can on the flora of the university farms, the university campus, and the adjoining suburbs. For a decade I have kept, for pastime, a record of the wild plant species in first bloom on these two diverse areas:

Species First Blooming in	Suburb and Campus	Backward Farm
April	14	26
May	29	59
June	43	70
July	25	56
August	9	14
September	0	1
Total visual diet	120	226

It is apparent that the backward farmer's eye is nearly twice as well fed as the eye of the university student or businessman. Of course neither sees his flora as yet, so we are confronted by the two alternatives already mentioned: either insure the continued blindness of the populace, or examine the question whether we cannot have both progress and plants.

The shrinkage in the flora is due to a combination of clean-farming, woodlot grazing, and good roads. Each of these necessary changes of course requires a larger reduction in the acreage available for wild plants, but none of them requires, or benefits by, the erasure of species from whole farms, townships, or counties. There are idle spots on every farm, and every highway is bordered by an idle strip as long as it is; keep cow, plow, and mower out of these idle spots, and the full native flora, plus dozens of interesting stowaways from foreign parts, could be part of the normal environment of every citizen.

The outstanding conservator of the prairie flora, ironically enough, knows little and cares less about such frivolities: it is the railroad with its fenced right-of-way. Many of these railroad fences were erected before the prairie had been plowed. Within these linear reservations, oblivious of cinders, soot, and annual clean-up fires, the prairie flora still splashes its calendar of colors, from pink shooting-star in May to blue aster in October. I have long wished to confront some hard-boiled railway president with the physical evidence of his soft-heartedness. I have not done so because I haven't met one.

The railroads of course use flame-throwers and chemical sprays to clear the track of weeds, but the cost of such necessary clearance is still too high to extend it much beyond the actual rails. Perhaps further improvements are in the offing.

The erasure of a human subspecies is largely painless—to us—if we know little enough about it. A dead Chinaman is of little import to us whose awareness of things Chinese is bounded by an occasional dish of chow mein. We grieve only for what we know. The erasure of Silphium from western Dane County is no cause for grief if one knows it only as a name in a botany book.

Silphium first became a personality to me when I tried to dig one up to move to my farm. It was like digging an oak sapling. After half an hour of hot grimy labor the root was still enlarging, like a great vertical sweet-potato. As far as I know, that Silphium root went clear through to bedrock. I got no Silphium, but I learned by what elaborate underground strategems it contrives to weather the prairie drouths.

I next planted Silphium seeds, which are large, meaty, and taste like sunflower seeds. They came up promptly, but after five years of waiting the seedlings are still juvenile, and have not yet borne a flower-stalk. Perhaps it takes a decade for a Silphium to reach flowering age; how old, then, was my pet plant in the cemetery? It may have been older than the oldest tombstone, which is dated 1850. Perhaps it watched the fugitive Black Hawk retreat from the Madison lakes to the Wisconsin River; it stood on the route of that famous march. Certainly it saw the successive funerals of the local pioneers as they retired, one by one, to their repose beneath the bluestem.

I once saw a power shovel, while digging a roadside ditch, sever the 'sweet-potato' root of a Silphium plant. The root soon sprouted new leaves, and eventually it again produced a flower stalk. This explains why this plant, which never invades new ground, is nevertheless sometimes seen on recently graded roadsides. Once established, it apparently withstands almost any kind of mutilation except continued grazing, mowing, or plowing.

Why does Silphium disappear from grazed areas? I once saw a farmer turn his cows into a virgin prairie meadow previously used only sporadically for mowing wild hay. The cows cropped the Silphium to the ground before any other plant was visibly eaten at all. One can imagine that the buffalo once had the same preference for Silphium, but he brooked no fences to confine his nibblings all summer long to one meadow. In short, the buffalo's pasturing was discontinuous, and therefore tolerable to Silphium.

It is a kind providence that has withheld a sense of history from the thousands of species of plants and animals that have exterminated each other to build the present world. The same kind providence now withholds it from us. Few grieved when the last buffalo left Wisconsin, and few will grieve when the last Silphium follows him to the lush prairies of the never-never land.

August

The Green Pasture

Some paintings become famous because, being durable, they are viewed by successive generations, in each of which are likely to be found a few appreciative eyes.

I know a painting so evanescent that it is seldom viewed at all, except by some wandering deer. It is a river who wields the brush, and it is the same river who, before I can bring my friends to view his work, erases it forever from human view. After that it exists only in my mind's eye.

Like other artists, my river is temperamental; there is no predicting when the mood to paint will come upon him, or how long it will last. But in midsummer, when the great white fleets cruise the sky for day after flawless day, it is worth strolling down to the sandbars just to see whether he has been at work.

The work begins with a broad ribbon of silt brushed thinly on the sand of a receding shore. As this dries slowly in the sun, goldfinches bathe in its pools, and deer, herons, killdeers, raccoons, and turtles cover it with a lacework of tracks. There is no telling, at this stage, whether anything further will happen.

But when I see the silt ribbon turning green with Eleocharis, I watch closely thereafter, for this is the sign that the river is in a painting mood. Almost overnight the Eleocharis

becomes a thick turf, so lush and so dense that the meadow mice from the adjoining upland cannot resist the temptation. They move *en masse* to the green pasture, and apparently spend the nights rubbing their ribs in its velvety depths. A maze of neatly tended mouse-trails bespeaks their enthusiasm. The deer walk up and down in it, apparently just for the pleasure of feeling it underfoot. Even a stay-at-home mole has tunneled his way across the dry bar to the Eleocharis ribbon, where he can heave and hump the verdant sod to his heart's content.

At this stage the seedlings of plants too numerous to count and too young to recognize spring to life from the damp warm sand under the green ribbon.

To view the painting, give the river three more weeks of solitude, and then visit the bar on some bright morning just after the sun has melted the daybreak fog. The artist has now laid his colors, and sprayed them with dew. The Eleocharis sod, greener than ever, is now spangled with blue mimulus, pink dragon-head, and the milk-white blooms of Sagittaria. Here and there a cardinal flower thrusts a red spear skyward. At the head of the bar, purple ironweeds and pale pink joe-pyes stand tall against the

wall of willows. And if you have come quietly and humbly, as you should to any spot that can be beautiful only once, you may surprise a fox-red deer, standing knee-high in the garden of his delight.

Do not return for a second view of the green pasture, for there is none. Either falling water has dried it out, or rising water has scoured the bar to its original austerity of clean sand. But in your mind you may hang up your picture, and hope that in some other summer the mood to paint may come upon the river.

September

The Choral Copse

By September, the day breaks with little help from birds. A song sparrow may give a single half-hearted song, a woodcock may twitter overhead *en route* to his daytime thicket, a barred owl may terminate the night's argument with one last wavering call, but few other birds have anything to say or sing about.

It is on some, but not all, of these misty autumn daybreaks that one may hear the chorus of the quail. The silence is suddenly broken by a dozen contralto voices, no longer able to restrain their praise of the day to come. After a brief minute or two, the music closes as suddenly as it began.

There is a peculiar virtue in the music of elusive birds. Songsters that sing from topmost boughs are easily seen and as easily forgotten; they have the mediocrity of the obvious. What one remembers is the invisible hermit thrush pouring silver chords from impenetrable shadows; the soaring crane trumpeting from behind a cloud; the prairie chicken booming from the mists of nowhere; the quail's Ave Maria in the hush of dawn. No naturalist has even seen the choral act, for the covey is still on its invisible roost in the grass, and any attempt to approach automatically induces silence.

In June it is completely predictable that the robin will give voice when the light intensity reaches 0.01 candle power, and that the bedlam of other singers will follow in pre-

dictable sequence. In autumn, on the other hand, the robin is silent, and it is quite unpredictable whether the covey-chorus will occur at all. The disappointment I feel on these mornings of silence perhaps shows that things hoped for have a higher value than things assured. The hope of hearing quail is worth half a dozen risings-in-the-dark. My farm always has one or more coveys in autumn, but the daybreak chorus is usually distant. I think this is because the coveys prefer to roost as far as possible from the dog, whose interest in quail is even more ardent than my own. One October dawn, however, as I sat sipping coffee by the outdoor fire, a chorus burst into song hardly a stone's throw away. They had roosted under a white-pine copse, possibly to stay dry during the heavy dews.

We felt honored by this daybreak hymn sung almost at our doorstep. Somehow the blue autumnal needles on those pines became thenceforth bluer, and the red carpet of dewberry under those pines became even redder.

October

Smoky Gold

There are two kinds of hunting: ordinary hunting, and ruffed-grouse hunting.

There are two places to hunt grouse: ordinary places, and Adams County.

There are two times to hunt in Adams: ordinary times, and when the tamaracks are smoky gold. This is written for those luckless ones who have never stood, gun empty and mouth agape, to watch the golden needles come sifting down, while the feathery-rocket that knocked them off sails unscathed into the jackpines.

The tamaracks change from green to yellow when the first frosts have brought woodcock, fox sparrows, and juncos out of the north. Troops of robins are stripping the last white berries from the dogwood thickets, leaving the empty stems as a pink haze against the hill. The creekside alders have shed their leaves, exposing here and there an eyeful of holly. Brambles are aglow, lighting your footsteps grouseward.

The dog knows what is grouseward better than you do. You will do well to follow him closely, reading from the cock of his ears the story the breeze is telling. When at last he stops stock-still, and says with a sideward glance, 'Well, get ready,' the question is, ready for what? A twittering woodcock, or the rising roar of a grouse, or perhaps only a rabbit? In this moment of uncertainty is condensed much of the virtue of grouse hunting. He who must know what to get ready for should go and hunt pheasants.

♫ ♫ ♫

Hunts differ in flavor, but the reasons are subtle. The sweetest hunts are stolen. To steal a hunt, either go far into the wilderness where no one has been, or else find some undiscovered place under everybody's nose.

Few hunters know that grouse exist in Adams County, for when they drive through it, they see only a waste of jackpines and scrub oaks. This is because the highway intersects a series of west-running creeks, each of which heads in a swamp, but drops to the river through dry sand-barrens. Naturally the northbound highway intersects these swampless barrens, but just above the highway, and behind the screen of dry scrub, every creeklet expands into a broad ribbon of swamp, a sure haven for grouse.

Here, come October, I sit in the solitude of my tamaracks and hear the hunters' cars roaring up the highway, hell-bent for the crowded counties to the north. I chuckle as I picture their dancing speedometers, their strained faces, their eager eyes glued on the northward horizon. At the noise of their passing, a cock grouse drums his defiance. My dog grins as we note his direction. That fellow, we agree, needs some exercise; we shall look him up presently.

The tamaracks grow not only in the swamp, but at the foot of the bordering upland, where springs break forth. Each spring has become choked with moss, which forms a boggy terrace. I call these terraces the hanging gardens, for out of their sodden muck the fringed gentians have lifted blue jewels. Such an October gentian, dusted with tamarack gold, is worth a full stop and a long look, even when the dog signals grouse ahead.

Between each hanging garden and the creekside is a moss-paved deer trail, handy for the hunter to follow, and for the flushed grouse to cross—in a split second. The question is whether the bird and the gun agree on how a second should be split. If they do not, the next deer that passes finds a pair of empty shells to sniff at, but no feathers.

Higher up the creeklet I encounter an abandoned farm. I try to read, from the age of the young jackpines marching across an old field, how long ago the luckless farmer found out that sand plains were meant to grow solitude, not corn. Jackpines tell tall tales to the unwary, for they put on several whorls of branches each year, instead of only one. I find a better chronometer in an elm seedling that now blocks the barn door. Its rings date back to the drouth of 1930. Since that year no man has carried milk out of this barn.

I wonder what this family thought about when their mortgage finally outgrew their crops, and thus gave the signal for their eviction. Many thoughts, like flying grouse, leave no trace of their passing, but some leave clues that outlast the decades. He who, in some unforgotten April, planted this lilac must have thought pleasantly of blooms for all the Aprils to come. She who used this washboard, its corrugations worn thin with many Mondays, may have wished for a cessation of all Mondays, and soon.

Musing on such questions, I become aware of the dog down by the spring, pointing patiently these many minutes. I walk up, apologizing for my inattention. Up twitters a woodcock, batlike, his salmon breast soaked in October sun. Thus goes the hunt.

It's hard on such a day to keep one's mind on grouse, for there are many distractions. I cross a buck track in the sand, and follow in idle curiosity. The track leads straight from one Jersey tea bush to another, with nipped twigs showing why.

This reminds me of my own lunch, but before I get it pulled out of my game pocket, I see a circling hawk, high skyward, needing identification. I wait till he banks and shows his red tail.

I reach again for the lunch, but my eye catches a peeled popple. Here a buck has rubbed off his itchy velvet. How long ago? The exposed wood is already brown; I conclude that horns must therefore be clean by now.

I reach again for the lunch, but am interrupted by an excited yawp from the dog, and a crash of bushes in the swamp. Out springs a buck, flag aloft, horns shining, his coat a sleek blue. Yes, the popple told the truth.

This time I get the lunch all the way out and sit down to eat. A chickadee watches me, and grows confidential about *his* lunch. He doesn't say what he ate, perhaps it was cool turgid ant-eggs, or some other avian equivalent of cold roast grouse.

Lunch over, I regard a phalanx of young tamaracks, their golden lances thrusting skyward. Under each the needles of yesterday fall to earth building a blanket of smoky gold; at the tip of each the bud of tomorrow, preformed, poised, awaits another spring.

Too Early

Getting up too early is a vice habitual in horned owls, stars, geese, and freight trains. Some hunters acquire it from geese, and some coffee pots from hunters. It is strange that of all the multitude of creatures who must rise in the morning at some time, only these few should have discovered the most pleasant and least useful time for doing it.

Orion must have been the original mentor of the too-early company, for it is he who signals for too-early rising. It is time when Orion has passed west of the zenith about as far as one should lead a teal.

Early risers feel at ease with each other, perhaps because, unlike those who sleep late, they are given to understatement of their own achievements. Orion, the most widely traveled, says literally nothing. The coffee pot, from its first soft gurgle, underclaims the virtues of what simmers within. The owl, in his trisyllabic commentary, plays down the story of the night's murders. The goose on the bar, rising briefly to a point of order in some inaudible anserine debate, lets fall no hint that he speaks with the authority of all the far hills and the sea.

The freight, I admit, is hardly reticent about his own importance, yet even he has a kind of modesty: his eye is single to his own noisy business, and he never comes roaring into somebody else's camp. I feel a deep security in this single-mindedness of freight trains.

☆ ☆ ☆

To arrive too early in the marsh is an adventure in pure listening; the ear roams at will among the noises of the night, without let or hindrance from hand or eye. When you hear a mallard being audibly enthusiastic about his soup, you are free to picture a score guzzling among the duckweeds. When one widgeon squeals, you may postulate a squadron without fear of visual contradiction. And when a flock of bluebills, pitching pondward, tears the dark silk of heaven in one long rending nose-dive, you catch your breath at the sound, but there is nothing to see except stars. This same performance, in daytime, would have to be looked at, shot at, missed, and then hurriedly fitted with an alibi. Nor could daylight add anything to your mind's eye picture of quivering wings, ripping the firmament neatly into halves.

The hour of listening ends when the fowl depart on muted wings for wider safer waters, each flock a blur against the graying east.

Like many another treaty of restraint, the pre-dawn pact lasts only as long as darkness humbles the arrogant. It would seem as if the sun were responsible for the daily retreat of reticence from the world At any rate, by the time the mists are white over the lowlands, every rooster is bragging *ad lib,* and every corn shock is pretending to be twice as tall as any corn that ever grew. By sun-up every squirrel is exaggerating some fancied indignity to his person, and every jay proclaiming with false emotion about supposititious dangers to society, at this very moment discovered by him. Distant crows are berating a hypothetical owl, just to tell the world how vigilant crows are, and a pheasant cock, musing perhaps on his philanderings of bygone days, beats the air with his wings and tells the world in raucous warning that he owns this marsh and all the hens in it.

Nor are all these illusions of grandeur confined to the birds and beasts. By breakfast

time come the honks, horns, shouts, and whistles of the awakened farmyard, and finally, at evening, the drone of an untended radio. Then everybody goes to bed to relearn the lessons of the night.

Red Lanterns

One way to hunt partridge is to make a plan, based on logic and probabilities, of the terrain to be hunted. This will take you over the ground where the birds ought to be.

Another way is to wander, quite aimlessly, from one red lantern to another. This will likely take you where the birds actually are. The lanterns are blackberry leaves, red in October sun.

Red lanterns have lighted my way on many a pleasant hunt in many a region, but I think that blackberries must first have learned how to glow in the sand counties of central Wisconsin. Along the little boggy streams of these friendly wastes, called poor by those whose own lights barely flicker, the blackberries burn richly red on every sunny day from first frost to the last day of the season. Every woodcock and every partridge has his private solarium under these briars. Most hunters, not knowing this, wear themselves out in the briarless scrub, and, returning home birdless, leave the rest of us in peace.

By 'us' I mean the birds, the stream, the dog, and myself. The stream is a lazy one; he winds through the alders as if he would rather stay here than reach the river. So would I. Every one of his hairpin hesitations means that much more streambank where hillside briars adjoin dank beds of frozen ferns and jewelweeds on the boggy bottom.

No partridge can long absent himself from such a place, nor can I. Partridge hunting, then, is a creekside stroll, upwind, from one briar patch to another.

The dog, when he approaches the briars, looks around to make sure I am within gun-shot. Reassured, he advances with stealthy caution, his wet nose screening a hundred scents for that one scent, the potential presence of which gives life and meaning to the whole landscape. He is the prospector of the air, perpetually searching its strata for olfactory gold. Partridge scent is the gold standard that relates his world to mine.

My dog, by the way, thinks I have much to learn about partridges, and, being a pro-fessional naturalist, I agree. He persists in tutoring me, with the calm patience of a professor of logic, in the art of drawing deductions from an educated nose. I delight in seeing him deduce a conclusion, in the form of a point, from data that are obvious to him, but speculative to my unaided eye. Perhaps he hopes his dull pupil will one day learn to smell.

Like other dull pupils, I know when the professor is right, even though I do not know why. I check my gun and walk in. Like any good professor, the dog never laughs when I miss, which is often. He gives me just one look, and proceeds up the stream in quest of another grouse.

Following one of these banks, one walks astride two landscapes, the hillside one hunts from, and the bottom the dog hunts in. There is a special charm in treading soft dry carpets of Lycopodium to flush birds out of the bog, and the first test of a partridge dog is his willingness to do the wet work while you parallel him on the dry bank.

A special problem arises where the belt of alders widens, and the dog disappears from view. Hurry at once to a knoll or point, where you stand stock-still, straining eye and ear to follow the dog. A sudden scattering of whitethroats may reveal his whereabouts.

Again you may hear him breaking a twig, or splashing in a wet spot, or plopping into

the creek. But when all sound ceases, be ready for instant action, for he is likely on

point. Listen now for the premonitory clucks a frightened partridge gives just before

flushing. Then follows the hurtling bird, or perhaps two of them, or I have known as

many as six, clucking and flushing one by one, each sailing high for his own destination

in the uplands. Whether one passes within gunshot is of course a matter of chance,

and you can compute the chance if you have time: 360 degrees divided by 30, or what-

ever segment of the circle your gun covers. Divide again by 3 or 4, which is your

chance of missing, and you have the probability of actual feathers in the hunting coat.

The second test of a good partridge dog is whether he reports for orders after such an episode. Sit down and talk it over with him while he pants. Then look for the next red lantern, and proceed with the hunt.

The October breeze brings my dog many scents other than grouse, each of which may lead to its own peculiar episode. When he points with a certain humorous expression of the ears, I know he has found a bedded rabbit. Once a dead-serious point yielded no bird, but still the dog stood frozen; in a tuft of sedge under his very nose was a fat sleeping coon, getting his share of October sun. At least once on each hunt the dog bays a skunk, usually in some denser-than-ordinary thicket of blackberries. Once the dog pointed in midstream: a whir of wings upriver, followed by three musical cries, told me he had interrupted a wood duck's dinner. Not infrequently he finds jacksnipe in heavily pastured alders, and lastly he may put out a deer, bedded for the day on a high streambank flanked by alder bog. Has the deer a poetical weakness for singing waters, or a practical liking for a bed that cannot be approached without making a noise? Judging by the indignant flick of his great white flag it might be either, or both.

Almost anything may happen between one red lantern and another.

ℐ ℐ ℐ

At sunset on the last day of the grouse season, every blackberry blows out his light. I do not understand how a mere bush can thus be infallibly informed about the Wisconsin statutes, nor have I ever gone back next day to find out. For the ensuing eleven months the lanterns glow only in recollection. I sometimes think that the other months were constituted mainly as a fitting interlude between Octobers, and I suspect that dogs, and perhaps grouse, share the same view.

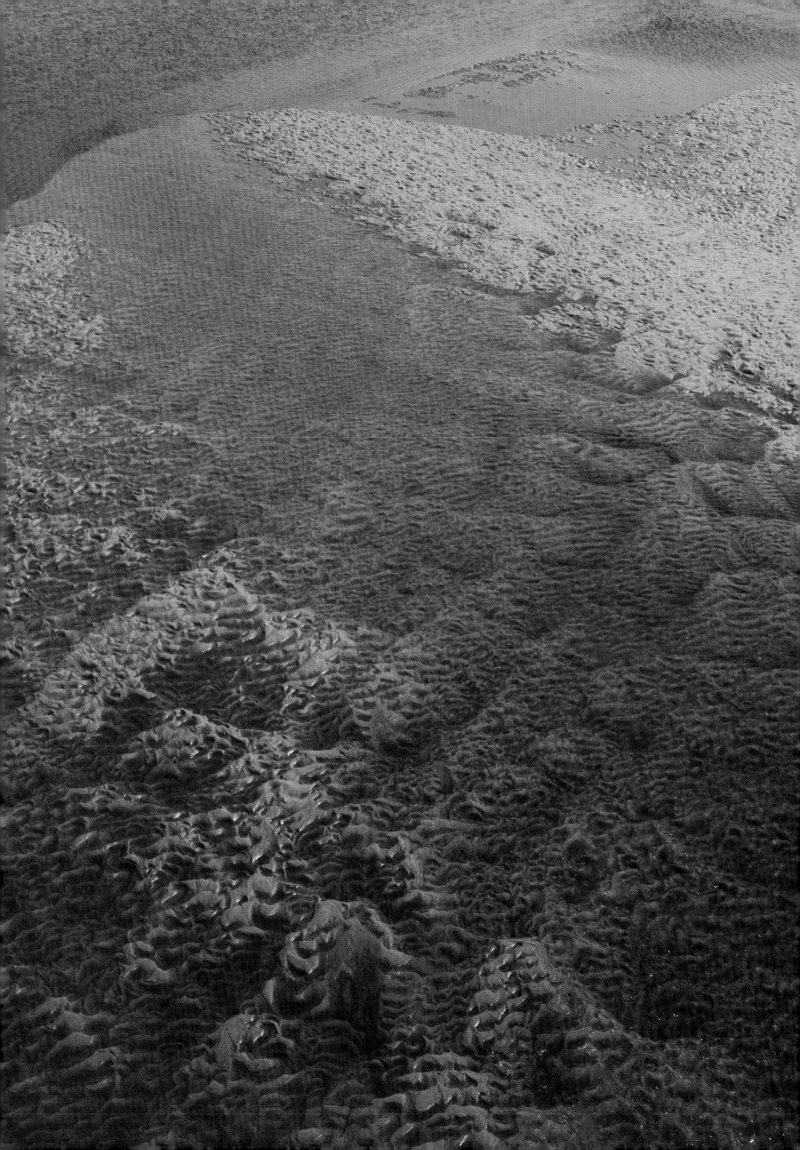

November

If I Were the Wind

The wind that makes music in November corn is in a hurry. The stalks hum, the loose husks whisk skyward in half-playful swirls, and the wind hurries on.

In the marsh, long windy waves surge across the grassy sloughs, beat against the far willows. A tree tries to argue, bare limbs waving, but there is no detaining the wind.

On the sandbar there is only wind, and the river sliding seaward. Every wisp of grass is drawing circles on the sand. I wander over the bar to a driftwood log, where I sit and listen to the universal roar, and to the tinkle of wavelets on the shore. The river is life-less: not a duck, heron, marshhawk, or gull but has sought refuge from wind.

🦢 🦢 🦢

Out of the clouds I hear a faint bark, as of a far-away dog. It is strange how the world cocks its ears at that sound, wondering. Soon it is louder: the honk of geese, invisible, but coming on.

The flock emerges from the low clouds, a tattered banner of birds, dipping and rising, blown up and blown down, blown together and blown apart, but advancing, the wind wrestling lovingly with each winnowing wing. When the flock is a blur in the far sky I hear the last honk, sounding taps for summer.

♫ ♫ ♫

It is warm behind the driftwood now, for the wind has gone with the geese. So would I—if I were the wind.

Axe-in-Hand

The Lord giveth, and the Lord taketh away, but He is no longer the only one to do so. When some remote ancestor of ours invented the shovel, he became a giver: he could plant a tree. And when the axe was invented, he became a taker: he could chop it down. Whoever owns land has thus assumed, whether he knows it or not, the divine functions of creating and destroying plants.

Other ancestors, less remote, have since invented other tools, but each of these, upon close scrutiny, proves to be either an elaboration of, or an accessory to, the original pair of basic implements. We classify ourselves into vocations, each of which either wields some particular tool, or sells it, or repairs it, or sharpens it, or dispenses advice on how to do so; by such division of labors we avoid responsibility for the misuse of any tool save our own. But there is one vocation—philosophy—which knows that all men, by what they think about and wish for, in effect wield all tools. It knows that men thus determine, by their manner of thinking and wishing, whether it is worth while to wield any.

♫ ♫ ♫

November is, for many reasons, the month for the axe. It is warm enough to grind an axe without freezing, but cold enough to fell a tree in comfort. The leaves are off the hardwoods, so that one can see just how the branches intertwine, and what growth occurred last summer. Without this clear view of treetops, one cannot be sure which tree, if any, needs felling for the good of the land.

I have read many definitions of what is a conservationist, and written not a few myself, but I suspect that the best one is written not with a pen, but with an axe. It is a matter of what a man thinks about while chopping, or while deciding what to chop. A conservationist is one who is humbly aware that with each stroke he is writing his signature on the face of his land. Signatures of course differ, whether written with axe or pen, and this is as it should be.

I find it disconcerting to analyze, *ex post facto,* the reasons behind my own axe-in-hand decisions. I find, first of all, that not all trees are created free and equal. Where a white pine and a red birch are crowding each other, I have an *a priori* bias; I always cut the birch to favor the pine. Why?

Well, first of all, I planted the pine with my shovel, whereas the birch crawled in under the fence and planted itself. My bias is thus to some extent paternal, but this cannot be the whole story, for if the pine were a natural seedling like the birch, I would value it even more. So I must dig deeper for the logic, if any, behind my bias.

The birch is an abundant tree in my township and becoming more so, whereas pine is scarce and becoming scarcer; perhaps my bias is for the underdog. But what would I do if my farm were further north, where pine is abundant and red birch is scarce? I confess I don't know. My farm is here.

The pine will live for a century, the birch for half that; do I fear that my signature will fade? My neighbors have planted no pines but all have many birches; am I snobbish about having a woodlot of distinction? The pine stays green all winter, the birch punches the clock in October; do I favor the tree that, like myself, braves the winter wind? The pine will shelter a grouse but the birch will feed him; do I consider bed more important than board? The pine will ultimately bring ten dollars a thousand, the birch two dollars; have I an eye on the bank? All of these possible reasons for my bias seem to carry some weight, but none of them carries very much.

So I try again, and here perhaps is something; under this pine will ultimately grow a trailing arbutus, an Indian pipe, a pyrola, or a twin flower, whereas under the birch a bottle gentian is about the best to be hoped for. In this pine a pileated woodpecker will ultimately chisel out a nest; in the birch a hairy will have to suffice. In this pine the wind will sing for me in April, at which time the birch is only rattling naked twigs. These possible reasons for my bias carry weight, but why? Does the pine stimulate my imagination and my hopes more deeply than the birch does? If so, is the difference in the trees, or in me?

The only conclusion I have ever reached is that I love all trees, but I am in love with pines.

As I said, November is the month for the axe, and, as in other love affairs, there is skill in the exercise of bias. If the birch stands south of the pine, and is taller, it will shade the pine's leader in the spring, and thus discourage the pine weevil from laying her eggs there. Birch competition is a minor affliction compared with this weevil, whose progeny kill the pine's leader and thus deform the tree. It is interesting to meditate that this

insect's preference for squatting in the sun determines not only her own continuity as a species, but also the future figure of my pine, and my own success as a wielder of axe and shovel.

Again, if a drouthy summer follows my removal of the birch's shade, the hotter soil may offset the lesser competition for water, and my pine be none the better for my bias.

Lastly, if the birch's limbs rub the pine's terminal buds during a wind, the pine will surely be deformed, and the birch must either be removed regardless of other considerations, or else it must be pruned of limbs each winter to a height greater than the pine's prospective summer growth.

Such are the pros and cons the wielder of an axe must foresee, compare, and decide upon with the calm assurance that his bias will, on the average, prove to be something more than good intentions.

The wielder of an axe has as many biases as there are species of trees on his farm. In the course of the years he imputes to each species, from his responses to their beauty or utility, and their responses to his labors for or against them, a series of attributes that constitute a character. I am amazed to learn what diverse characters different men impute to one and the same tree.

Thus to me the aspen is in good repute because he glorifies October and he feeds my grouse in winter, but to some of my neighbors he is a mere weed, perhaps because he sprouted so vigorously in the stump lots their grandfathers were attempting to clear. (I cannot sneer at this, for I find myself disliking the elms whose resproutings threaten my pines.)

Again, the tamarack is to me a favorite second only to white pine, perhaps because he is nearly extinct in my township (underdog bias), or because he sprinkles gold on October grouse (gunpowder bias), or because he sours the soil and enables it to grow the loveliest of our orchids, the showy lady's-slipper. On the other hand, foresters have excommunicated the tamarack because he grows too slowly to pay compound interest. In order to clinch this dispute, they also mention that he succumbs periodically to epizootics of saw-fly, but this is fifty years hence for my tamaracks, so I shall let my grandson worry about it. Meanwhile my tamaracks are growing so lustily that my spirits soar with them, skyward.

To me an ancient cottonwood is the greatest of trees because in his youth he shaded the buffalo and wore a halo of pigeons, and I like a young cottonwood because he may some day become ancient. But the farmer's wife (and hence the farmer) despises all cottonwoods because in June the female tree clogs the screens with cotton. The modern dogma is comfort at any cost.

I find my biases more numerous than those of my neighbors because I have individual likings for many species that they lump under one aspersive category: brush. Thus I like the wahoo, partly because deer, rabbits, and mice are so avid to eat his square twigs and green bark and partly because his cerise berries glow so warmly against November snow. I like the red dogwood because he feeds October robins, and the prickly ash because my woodcock take their daily sunbath under the shelter of his thorns. I like the hazel because his October purple feeds my eye, and because his November catkins feed my deer and grouse. I like the bittersweet because my father did, and because the deer, on the 1st of July of each year, begin suddenly to eat the new leaves, and I have learned to predict this event to my guests. I cannot dislike a plant that enables me, a mere professor, to blossom forth annually as a successful seer and prophet.

It is evident that our plant biases are in part traditional. If your grandfather liked hickory nuts, you will like the hickory tree because your father told you to. If, on the other hand, your grandfather burned a log carrying a poison ivy vine and recklessly stood in the smoke, you will dislike the species, no matter with what crimson glories it warms your eyes each fall.

It is also evident that our plant biases reflect not only vocations but avocations, with a delicate allocation of priority as between industry and indolence. The farmer who would rather hunt grouse than milk cows will not dislike hawthorn, no matter if it does invade his pasture. The coon-hunter will not dislike basswood, and I know of quail hunters who bear no grudge against ragweed, despite their annual bout with hayfever. Our biases are indeed a sensitive index to our affections, our tastes, our loyalties, our generosities, and our manner of wasting weekends.

Be that as it may, I am content to waste mine, in November, with axe in hand.

A Mighty Fortress

Every farm woodland, in addition to yielding lumber, fuel, and posts, should provide its owner a liberal education. This crop of wisdom never fails, but it is not always harvested. I here record some of the many lessons I have learned in my own woods.

♫ ♫ ♫

Soon after I bought the woods a decade ago, I realized that I had bought almost as many tree diseases as I had trees. My woodlot is riddled by all the ailments wood is heir to. I began to wish that Noah, when he loaded up the Ark, had left the tree diseases behind. But it soon became clear that these same diseases made my woodlot a mighty fortress, unequaled in the whole county.

My woods is headquarters for a family of coons; few of my neighbors have any. One Sunday in November, after a new snow, I learned why. The fresh track of a coon-hunter and his hound led up to a half-uprooted maple, under which one of my coons had taken refuge. The frozen snarl of roots and earth was too rocky to chop and too tough to dig; the holes under the roots were too numerous to smoke out. The hunter had quit coonless because a fungus disease had weakened the roots of the maple. The tree, half tipped over by a storm, offers an impregnable fortress for coondom. Without this 'bombproof' shelter, my seed stock of coons would be cleaned out by hunters each year.

My woods houses a dozen ruffed grouse, but during periods of deep snow my grouse shift to my neighbor's woods, where there is better cover. However, I always retain as many grouse as I have oaks wind-thrown by summer storms. These summer windfalls keep their dried leaves, and during snows each such windfall harbors a grouse. The droppings show that each grouse roosts, feeds, and loafs for the duration of the storm within the narrow confines of his leafy camouflage, safe from wind, owl, fox, and hunter. The cured oak leaves not only serve as cover, but, for some curious reason, are relished as food by the grouse.

These oak windfalls are, of course, diseased trees. Without disease, few oaks would break off, and hence few grouse would have down tops to hide in.

Diseased oaks also provide another apparently delectable grouse food: oak galls. A gall is a diseased growth of new twigs that have been stung by a gall-wasp while tender and succulent. In October my grouse are often stuffed with oak galls.

Each year the wild bees load up one of my hollow oaks with combs, and each year trespassing honey-hunters harvest the honey before I do. This is partly because they are more skillful than I am in 'lining up' the bee trees, and partly because they use nets, and hence are able to work before the bees become dormant in fall. But for heart-rots, there would be no hollow oaks to furnish wild bees with oaken hives.

During high years of the cycle, there is a plague of rabbits in my woods. They eat the bark and twigs off almost every kind of tree or bush I am trying to encourage, and ignore almost every kind I should like to have less of. (When the rabbit-hunter plants himself a grove of pines or an orchard, the rabbit somehow ceases to be a game animal and becomes a pest instead.)

The rabbit, despite his omnivorous appetite, is an epicure in some respects. He always prefers a hand-planted pine, maple, apple, or wahoo to a wild one. He also insists that certain salads be preconditioned before he deigns to eat them. Thus he spurns red dogwood until it is attacked by oyster-shell scale, after which the bark becomes a delicacy, to be eagerly devoured by all the rabbits in the neighborhood.

A flock of a dozen chickadees spends the year in my woods. In winter, when we are harvesting diseased or dead trees for our fuel wood, the ring of the axe is dinner gong for the chickadee tribe. They hang in the offing waiting for the tree to fall, offering pert commentary on the slowness of our labor. When the tree at last is down, and the wedges begin to open up its contents, the chickadees draw up their white napkins and fall to. Every slab of dead bark is, to them, a treasury of eggs, larvae, and cocoons.

For them every ant-tunneled heartwood bulges with milk and honey. We often stand a fresh split against a near-by tree just to see the greedy chicks mop up the ant-eggs. It lightens our labor to know that they, as well as we, derive aid and comfort from the fragrant riches of newly split oak.

But for diseases and insect pests, there would likely be no food in these trees, and hence no chickadees to add cheer to my woods in winter.

Many other kinds of wildlife depend on tree diseases. My pileated woodpeckers chisel living pines, to extract fat grubs from the diseased heartwood. My barred owls find surcease from crows and jays in the hollow heart of an old basswood; but for this diseased tree their sundown serenade would probably be silenced. My wood ducks nest in hollow trees; every June brings its brood of downy ducklings to my woodland slough. All squirrels depend, for permanent dens, on a delicately balanced equilibrium between a rotting cavity and the scar tissue with which the tree attempts to close the wound. The squirrels referee the contest by gnawing out the scar tissue when it begins unduly to shrink the amplitude of their front door.

The real jewel of my disease-ridden woodlot is the prothonotary warbler. He nests in an old woodpecker hole, or other small cavity, in a dead snag overhanging water. The flash of his gold-and-blue plumage amid the dank decay of the June woods is in itself proof that dead trees are transmuted into living animals, and vice versa. When you doubt the wisdom of this arrangement, take a look at the prothonotary.

December

Home Range

The wild things that live on my farm are reluctant to tell me, in so many words, how much of my township is included within their daily or nightly beat. I am curious about this, for it gives me the ratio between the size of their universe and the size of mine, and it conveniently begs the much more important question, who is the more thoroughly acquainted with the world in which he lives?

Like people, my animals frequently disclose by their actions what they decline to divulge in words. It is difficult to predict when and how one of these disclosures will come to light.

ഗ ഗ ഗ

The dog, being no hand with an axe, is free to hunt while the rest of us are making wood. A sudden *yip-yip-yip* gives us notice that a rabbit, flushed from his bed in the grass, is headed elsewhere in a hurry. He makes a beeline for a woodpile a quarter-mile distant, where he ducks between two corded stacks, a safe gunshot ahead of his pursuer. The dog, after leaving a few symbolic toothmarks on the hard oak, gives it up and resumes his search for some less canny cottontail, and we resume our chopping.

This little episode tells me that this rabbit is familiar with all of the ground between his bed in the meadow and his blitz-cellar under the woodpile. How else the beeline? This rabbit's home range is at least a quarter-mile in extent.

The chickadees that visit our feeding station are trapped and banded each winter. Some of our neighbors also feed chickadees, but none band them. By noticing the furthest points from my feeder at which banded chickadees are seen, we have learned that the home range of our flock is half a mile across in winter, but that it includes only areas protected from wind.

In summer, when the flock has dispersed for nesting, banded birds are seen at greater distances, often mated with unbanded birds. At this season the chickadees pay no heed to wind, often being found in open wind-swept places.

The fresh tracks of three deer, clear in yesterday's snow, pass through our woods. I follow the tracks backward and find a cluster of three beds, clear of snow, in the big willow thicket on the sandbar.

I then follow the tracks forward; they lead to my neighbor's cornfield, where the deer have pawed waste corn out of the snow, and also tousled one of the shocks. The tracks then lead back, by another route, to the sandbar. *En route* the deer have pawed at some grass tufts, nuzzling for the tender green sprouts within, and they have also drunk at a spring. My picture of the night's routine is complete. The over-all distance from bed to breakfast is a mile.

Our woods always harbors grouse, but one day last winter, after a deep and soft snow, I could find neither a grouse nor a track of one. I had about concluded that my birds had moved out, when my dog came to a point in the leafy top of an oak blown down last summer. Three grouse flushed out, one by one.

There were no tracks under or near the down top. Obviously these birds had flown in, but from where? Grouse must eat, especially in zero weather, so I examined the droppings for a clue. Among much unrecognizable debris I found bud-scales, and also the tough yellow skins of frozen nightshade berries.

In a thicket of young soft maple I had noticed, in summer, an abundant growth of nightshade. I went there and, after a search, found grouse tracks on a log . The birds had not waded the soft snow; they had walked the logs and picked the berries projecting here and there within their reach. This was a quarter-mile east of the down oak.

That evening, at sunset, I saw a grouse budding in a popple thicket a quarter-mile west. There were no tracks. This completed the story. These birds, for the duration of the soft snow, were covering their home range a-wing, not afoot, and the range was half a mile across.

♫ ♫ ♫

Science knows little about home range: how big it is at various seasons, what food and cover it must include, when and how it is defended against trespass, and whether ownership is an individual, family, or group affair. These are the fundamentals of animal economics, or ecology. Every farm is a textbook on animal ecology; woodsmanship is the translation of the book.

Pines above the Snow

Acts of creation are ordinarily reserved for gods and poets, but humbler folk may circumvent this restriction if they know how. To plant a pine, for example, one need be neither god nor poet; one need only own a shovel. By virtue of this curious loophole in the rules, any clodhopper may say: Let there be a tree—and there will be one.

If his back be strong and his shovel sharp, there may eventually be ten thousand. And in the seventh year he may lean upon his shovel, and look upon his trees, and find them good.

God passed on his handiwork as early as the seventh day, but I notice He has since been rather noncommittal about its merits. I gather either that He spoke too soon, or that trees stand more looking upon than do fig leaves and firmaments.

♫ ♫ ♫

Why is the shovel regarded as a symbol of drudgery? Perhaps because most shovels are dull. Certainly all drudges have dull shovels, but I am uncertain which of these two facts is cause and which effect. I only know that a good file, vigorously wielded, makes my shovel sing as it slices the mellow loam. I am told there is music in the sharp plane, the sharp chisel, and the sharp scalpel, but I hear it best in my shovel; it hums in my wrists as I plant a pine. I suspect that the fellow who tried so hard to strike one clear note upon the harp of time chose too difficult an instrument.

It is well that the planting season comes only in spring, for moderation is best in all things, even shovels. During the other months you may watch the process of becoming a pine.

The pine's new year begins in May, when the terminal bud becomes 'the candle.' Whoever coined that name for the new growth had subtlety in his soul. 'The candle' sounds like a platitudinous reference to obvious facts: the new shoot is waxy, upright, brittle. But he who lives with pines knows that candle has a deeper meaning, for at its tip burns the eternal flame that lights a path into the future. May after May my pines follow their candles skyward, each headed straight for the zenith, and each meaning to get there if only there be years enough before the last trumpet blows. It is a very old pine who at last forgets which of his many candles is the most important, and thus flattens his crown against the sky. You may forget, but no pine of your own planting will do so in your lifetime.

If you are thriftily inclined, you will find pines congenial company, for, unlike the hand-to-mouth hardwoods, they never pay current bills out of current earnings; they live solely on their savings of the year before. In fact every pine carries an open bankbook, in which his cash balance is recorded by 30 June of each year. If, on that date, his completed candle has developed a terminal cluster of ten or twelve buds, it means that he has salted away enough rain and sun for a two-foot or even a three-foot thrust skyward next spring. If there are only four or six buds, his thrust will be a lesser one, but he will nevertheless wear that peculiar air that goes with solvency.

Hard years, of course, come to pines as they do to men, and these are recorded as shorter thrusts, i.e. shorter spaces between the successive whorls of branches. These spaces, then, are an autobiography that he who walks with trees may read at will. In order to date a hard year correctly, you must always subtract one from the year of lesser growth. Thus the 1937 growth was short in all pines; this records the universal drouth of 1936. On the other hand the 1941 growth was long in all pines; perhaps they saw the shadow of things to come, and made a special effort to show the world that pines still know where they are going, even though men do not.

When one pine shows a short year but his neighbors do not, you may safely interpolate some purely local or individual adversity: a fire scar, a gnawing meadowmouse, a windburn, or some local bottleneck in that dark laboratory we call the soil.

✑ ✑ ✑

There is much small-talk and neighborhood gossip among pines. By paying heed to this chatter, I learn what has transpired during the week when I am absent in town. Thus in March, when the deer frequently browse white pines, the height of the browsings tells me how hungry they are. A deer full of corn is too lazy to nip branches more than four feet above the ground; a really hungry deer rises on his hind legs and nips as high as eight feet. Thus I learn the gastronomic status of the deer without seeing them, and I learn, without visiting his field, whether my neighbor has hauled in his cornshocks.

In May, when the new candle is tender and brittle as an asparagus shoot, a bird alighting on it will often break it off. Every spring I find a few such decapitated trees, each with its wilted candle lying in the grass. It is easy to infer what has happened, but in a decade of watching I have never once *seen* a bird break a candle. It is an object lesson: one need not doubt the unseen.

In June of each year a few white pines suddenly show wilted candles, which shortly thereafter turn brown and die. A pine weevil has bored into the terminal bud cluster and deposited eggs; the grubs, when hatched, bore down along the pith and kill the shoot. Such a leaderless pine is doomed to frustration, for the surviving branches disagree among themselves who is to head the skyward march. They all do, and as a consequence the tree remains a bush.

It is a curious circumstance that only pines in full sunlight are bitten by weevils; shaded pines are ignored. Such are the hidden uses of adversity.

In October my pines tell me, by their rubbed-off bark, when the bucks are beginning to 'feel their oats.' A jackpine about eight feet high, and standing alone, seems especially to incite in a buck the idea that the world needs prodding. Such a tree must perforce turn the other cheek also, and emerges much the worse for wear. The only element of justice in such combats is that the more the tree is punished, the more pitch the buck carries away on his not-so-shiny antlers.

The chit-chat of the woods is sometimes hard to translate. Once in midwinter I found in the droppings under a grouse roost some half-digested structures that I could not identify. They resembled miniature corncobs about half an inch long. I examined samples of every local grouse food I could think of, but without finding any clue to the origin of the 'cobs.' Finally I cut open the terminal bud of a jackpine, and in its core I found the anwer. The grouse had eaten the buds, digested the pitch, rubbed off the scales in his gizzard, and left the cob, which was, in effect, the forthcoming candle. One might say that this grouse had been speculating in jackpine 'futures.'

꿍 꿍 꿍

The three species of pine native to Wisconsin (white, red, and jack) differ radically in their opinions about marriageable age. The precocious jackpine sometimes blooms and bears cones a year or two after leaving the nursery, and a few of my 13-year-old jacks already boast of grandchildren. My 13-year-old reds first bloomed this year, but my whites have not yet bloomed; they adhere closely to the Anglo-Saxon doctrine of free, white, and twenty-one.

Were it not for this wide diversity in social outlook, my red squirrels would be much curtailed in their bill-of-fare. Each year in midsummer they start tearing up jackpine cones for the seeds, and no Labor-Day picnic ever scattered more hulls and rinds over the landscape than they do: under each tree the remains of their annual feast lie in piles and heaps. Yet there are always cones to spare, as attested by their progeny popping up among the goldenrods.

Few people know that pines bear flowers, and most of those who do are too prosy to see in this festival of bloom anything more than a routine biological function. All disillusioned folk should spend the second week in May in a pine woods, and such as wear glasses should take along an extra handkerchief. The prodigality of pine pollen should convince anyone of the reckless exuberance of the season, even when the song of the kinglet has failed to do so.

Young white pines usually thrive best in the absence of their parents. I know of whole woodlots in which the younger generation, even when provided with a place in the sun, is dwarfed and spindled by its elders. Again there are woodlots in which no such inhibition obtains. I wish I knew whether such differences lie in tolerance in the young, in the old, or in the soil.

Pines, like people, are choosy about their associates and do not succeed in suppressing their likes and dislikes. Thus there is an affinity between white pines and dewberries, between red pines and flowering spurge, between jackpines and sweet fern. When I plant a white pine in a dewberry patch, I can safely predict that within a year he will develop a husky cluster of buds, and that his new needles will show that bluish bloom which bespeaks health and congenial company. He will outgrow and outbloom his fellows planted on the same day, with the same care, in the same soil, but in the company of grass.

In October I like to walk among these blue plumes, rising straight and stalwart from the red carpet of dewberry leaves. I wonder whether they are aware of their state of well-being. I know only that I am.

Pines have earned the reputation of being 'evergreen' by the same device that governments use to achieve the appearance of perpetuity: overlapping terms of office. By taking on new needles on the new growth of each year, and discarding old needles at longer intervals, they have led the casual onlooker to believe that needles remain forever green.

Each species of pine has its own constitution, which prescribes a term of office for needles appropriate to its way of life. Thus the white pine retains its needles for a year and a half; the red and jackpines for two years and a half. Incoming needles take office in June, and outgoing needles write farewell addresses in October. All write the same thing, in the same tawny yellow ink, which by November turns brown. Then the needles fall, and are filed in the duff to enrich the wisdom of the stand. It is this accumulated wisdom that hushes the footsteps of whoever walks under pines.

It is in midwinter that I sometimes glean from my pines something more important than woodlot politics, and the news of the wind and weather. This is especially likely to happen on some gloomy evening when the snow has buried all irrelevant detail, and the hush of elemental sadness lies heavy upon every living thing. Nevertheless, my pines, each with his burden of snow, are standing ramrod-straight, rank upon rank, and in the dusk beyond I sense the presence of hundreds more. At such times I feel a curious transfusion of courage.

65290

To band a bird is to hold a ticket in a great lottery. Most of us hold tickets on our own survival, but we buy them from the insurance company, which knows too much to sell us a really sporting chance. It is an exercise in objectivity to hold a ticket on the banded sparrow that falleth, or on the banded chickadee that may some day re-enter your trap, and thus prove that he is still alive.

The tyro gets his thrill from banding new birds; he plays a kind of game against himself, striving to break his previous score for total numbers. But to the old-timer the banding of new birds becomes merely pleasant routine; the real thrill lies in the recapture of some bird banded long ago, some bird whose age, adventures, and previous condition of appetite are perhaps better known to you than to the bird himself.

Thus in our family, the question whether chickadee 65290 would survive for still another winter was, for five years, a sporting question of the first magnitude.

Beginning a decade ago, we have trapped and banded most of the chickadees on our farm each winter. In early winter, the traps yield mostly unbanded birds; these presumably are mostly the young of the year, which, once banded, can thereafter be 'dated.' As the winter wears on, unbanded birds cease to appear in the trap; we then know that the local population consists largely of marked birds. We can tell from the band numbers how many birds are present, and how many of these are survivors from each previous year of banding.

65290 was one of 7 chickadees constituting the 'class of 1937.' When he first entered our trap, he showed no visible evidence of genius. Like his classmates, his valor for suet was greater than his discretion. Like his classmates, he bit my finger while being taken out of the trap . When banded and released he fluttered up to a limb, pecked his new aluminum anklet in mild annoyance, shook his mussed feathers, cursed gently, and hurried away to catch up with the gang. It is doubtful whether he drew any philosophical deductions from his experience (such as 'all is not ants' eggs that glitters'), for he was caught again three times that same winter.

By the second winter our recaptures showed that the class of 7 had shrunk to 3, and by the third winter to 2. By the fifth winter 65290 was the sole survivor of his generation. Signs of genuis were still lacking, but of his extraordinary capacity for living, there was now historical proof.

During his sixth winter 65290 failed to reappear, and the verdict of 'missing in action' is now confirmed by his absence during four subsequent trappings.

At that, of 97 chicks banded during the decade, 65290 was the only one contriving to survive for five winters. Three reached 4 years, 7 reached 3 years, 19 reached 2 years, and 67 disappeared after their first winter. Hence if I were selling insurance to chicks, I could compute the premium with assurance. But this would raise the problem: in what currency would I pay the widows? I suppose in ants' eggs.

I know so little about birds that I can only speculate on why 65290 survived his fellows. Was he more clever in dodging his enemies? What enemies? A chickadee is almost too small to have any. That whimsical fellow called Evolution, having enlarged the dinosaur until he tripped over his own toes, tried shrinking the chickadee until he was just too big to be snapped up by flycatchers as an insect, and just too little to be pursued by hawks and owls as meat. Then he regarded his handiwork and laughed. Everyone laughs at so small a bundle of large enthusiasms.

The sparrow hawk, the screech owl, the shrike, and especially the midget saw-whet owl might find it worth while to kill a chickadee, but I've only once found evidence of actual murder: a screech-owl pellet contained one of my bands. Perhaps these small bandits have a fellow-feeling for midgets.

It seems likely that weather is the only killer so devoid of both humor and dimension as to kill a chickadee. I suspect that in the chickadee Sunday School two mortal sins are taught: thou shalt not venture into windy places in winter, thou shalt not get wet before a blizzard.

I learned the second commandment one drizzly winter dusk while watching a band of chicks going to roost in my woods. The drizzle came out of the south, but I could tell it would turn northwest and bitter cold before morning. The chicks went to bed in a dead oak, the bark of which had peeled and warped into curls, cups, and hollows of various sizes, shapes, and exposures. The bird selecting a roost dry against a south drizzle, but vulnerable to a north one, would surely be frozen by morning. The bird selecting a roost dry from all sides would awaken safe. This, I think, is the kind of wisdom that spells survival in chickdom, and accounts for 65290 and his like.

The chickadee's fear of windy places is easily deduced from his behavior. In winter he ventures away from woods only on calm days, and the distance varies inversely as the breeze. I know several wind-swept woodlots that are chickless all winter, but are freely used at all other seasons. They are wind-swept because cows have browsed out the undergrowth. To the steam-heated banker who mortgages the farmer who needs more cows who need more pasture, wind is a minor nuisance, except perhaps at the Flatiron corner. To the chickadee, winter wind is the boundary of the habitable world. If the chickadee had an office, the maxim over his desk would say: 'Keep calm.'

His behavior at the trap discloses the reason. Turn your trap so that he must enter with even a moderate wind at his tail, and all the king's horses cannot drag him to the bait. Turn it the other way, and your score may be good. Wind from behind blows cold and wet under the feathers, which are his portable roof and air-conditioner. Nuthatches, juncos, tree sparrows, and woodpeckers likewise fear winds from behind, but their heating plants and hence their wind tolerance are larger in the order named. Books on nature seldom mention wind; they are written behind stoves.

I suspect there is a third commandment in chickdom: thou shalt investigate every loud noise. When we start chopping in our woods, the chicks at once appear and stay until the felled trees or riven log has exposed new insect eggs or pupae for their delectation. The discharge of a gun will likewise summon chicks, but with less satisfactory dividends.

What served as their dinner bell before the day of axes, mauls, and guns? Presumably the crash of falling trees. In December 1940, an ice-storm felled an extraordinary number of dead snags and living limbs in our woods. Our chicks scoffed at the trap for a month, being replete with the dividends of the storm.

65290 has long since gone to his reward. I hope that in his new woods, great oaks full of ants' eggs keep falling all day long, with never a wind to ruffle his composure or take the edge off his appetite. And I hope that he still wears my band.

A phalanx of young tamaracks. About 1938.

Let there be a tree.

Great Possessions 1938.

Afterword

One winter day in 1935 my father, conveying a sense of excitement, bundled the family into the old sedan to visit a piece of land he had decided to buy (80 acres at eight dollars an acre). Wind and drifting snow made for slow travel, and often we five teen-agers found ourselves out in the drifts, shoulder to the car, lending aid to the laboring engine. Finally we were there.

Probably there is nothing bleaker than a worn-out and abandoned farm in a February ground blizzard. We found ourselves standing in a flat field, so poor that it could scarcely support marsh grass and a few scattered weeds, and facing a tumbledown shed filled with frozen cow manure and chicken droppings. What did my father see in this place that put the sparkle in his eyes? Dad was not a joker. He had a rich sense of humor, yet he tended to be silent, serious, driven by inner fires that we all sensed but only vaguely understood or shared. On this particular moment the understanding and sharing probably reached its lowest point as we stood shivering, gazing at Dad's treasure, waiting for a miracle or some great blinding revelation.

In time the revelation came, but only slowly, laboriously, and incrementally, on weekends over the next twelve years, as we worked and sweated and shared in the effort to restore this worn piece of land to life and health.

First was the need to provide a family shelter. Our choices were three. We could rebuild on the old stone foundation left by the fire probably set by the last owner as he walked away from his acres of shriveled corn and blowing sand. We might build something new. Father selected the chicken shed, which was later to be called the shack and to become our headquarters for weekend work. It also ultimately housed evening singing and guitar music, which probably had its roots in the Spanish genes passed on to us by Mother.

In making a shelter out of the chicken shed we gained our first insight: You don't have to know precisely where you are going, but if you become involved in making a start, the excitement is there. This was Father's way of teaching. He seldom told us anything directly unless it was in answer to a question. Father often raised questions himself, but not rhetorically, not with his own pet answers ready in his hip pocket. His were questions that forced us to probe our own minds until we came face to face with our ignorance. Knowing clearly what you *don't* know is the first step toward learning. He would light up whenever he got a good searching question from any of us, not because he had a handy answer, but because he saw learning in progress. He would also light up when any of us made a new observation. How well I remember the spring day when I rushed to him with the news that the martins had arrived. His warm smile said, "Ah, you noticed."

It is unlikely that Father started with a clear vision of what he was going to do with the land around the shack. But the attempt to rehabilitate it brought its own lessons, its own continuous self-renewal, and its own dedication to an increasingly sharper vision. The main questions without immediate answers were: What precisely *is* healthy land? What grew here before it was lumbered and "corned" to death? How do we win it back?

Aldo Leopold 1947.

The eternal battle against a smoky fireplace.

Aldo and Carl Leopold planting pines. About 1937.

As a trained forester, Father knew that just leaving abused land alone does not ensure its return to a state of health. And this was our ultimate objective. Prior to the coming of white men, the area had been mixed forest and prairie. This posed new questions. What is a forest? Certainly it is more than trees. What is a prairie? Certainly it is more than a sea of grass. Ultimately we did plant forty-eight thousand pines and experimented with plots of prairie plants.

Ever so slowly the landscape began to change. There were discouraging setbacks. For instance, Father's journal for July 19, 1936, records the following mortality in the first year's planting:

Norway pines	95% dead
White pines	99% dead
Mountain ash	100% dead
Tamaracks	50% dead

But with repeated plantings and a slow accumulation of experience about how to husband the seedlings, the survival rate improved. Also ever so slowly and painfully, without our being completely aware of it, all of us were learning something about ecology in perhaps the only way it can really be learned—in formulating the small questions. By making the observations, keeping the records, and performing the experiments, we began to discover the successful combinations of plants and animals that constitute a healthy land.

I know now a few small pieces of the answers to these questions, and I know clearly now why my father was basically a very humble man. It is a humbling thing to know important questions for which you have no answers.

Did Aldo Leopold truly visualize the deep pine-and-oak forest that now, forty years later, shelters deer and provides drumming logs for grouse? Did he visualize the lush native prairie with its big bluestem grass as high as I can reach, its myriad flowers blooming in succession from spring to autumn? Did he see the return of the sandhill cranes that now dance in the big marsh? Did he anticipate the battle now being waged to prevent the aspen and dogwood he planted from taking

Burning the fire break.

Hauling Good Oak.

Rest! cries the chief sawyer, and we pause for breath.

over his prairie and marsh? Did he see a family that would never again view land casually? What did he see on that cold winter day in 1935?

Nina Leopold Bradley

May 1, 1977

Photographer Identifications